my **revision** notes

CCEA GCSE

DIGITAL TECHNOLOGY

Siobhan Matthewson
Gerry Lynch
Margaret Debbadi

HODDER
EDUCATION
AN HACHETTE UK COMPANY

Photo on page 50 © Javier Larrea/Age fotostock/Alamy Stock Photo; the photo in the website on page 132 is © Shutterstock/Charlie Hutton.com.

Although every effort has been made to ensure that website addresses are correct at time of going to press, Hodder Education cannot be held responsible for the content of any website mentioned in this book. It is sometimes possible to find a relocated web page by typing in the address of the home page for a website in the URL window of your browser.

Hachette UK's policy is to use papers that are natural, renewable and recyclable products and made from wood grown in sustainable forests. The logging and manufacturing processes are expected to conform to the environmental regulations of the country of origin.

Orders: please contact Bookpoint Ltd, 130 Park Drive, Milton Park, Abingdon, Oxon OX14 4SE. Telephone: (44) 01235 827720. Fax: (44) 01235 400401. Email education@bookpoint.co.uk Lines are open from 9 a.m. to 5 p.m., Monday to Saturday, with a 24-hour message answering service. You can also order through our website: www.hoddereducation.co.uk

ISBN: 978 1 5104 2721 1

© Siobhan Matthewson, Gerry Lynch and Margaret Debbadi 2018

First published in 2018 by

Hodder Education,

An Hachette UK Company

Carmelite House

50 Victoria Embankment

London EC4Y 0DZ

www.hoddereducation.co.uk

Impression number   10 9 8 7 6 5 4 3

Year   2022 2021 2020 2019

Cover photo © Vladislav Ociacia/Getty Images/iStockphoto/Thinkstock

Typeset in India

Printed in India

A catalogue record for this title is available from the British Library.

Get the most from this book

Everyone has to decide his or her own revision strategy, but it is essential to review your work, learn it and test your understanding. These Revision Notes will help you to do that in a planned way, topic by topic. Use this book as the cornerstone of your revision and don't hesitate to write in it: personalise your notes and check your progress by ticking off each section as you revise.

Tick to track your progress

Use the revision planner on page 4 to plan your revision, topic by topic. Tick each box when you have:

- revised and understood a topic
- tested yourself
- practised the exam questions and checked your answers.

You can also keep track of your revision by ticking off each topic heading in the book. You may find it helpful to add your own notes as you work through each topic.

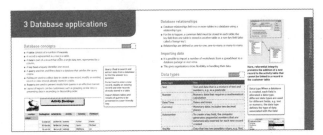

Features to help you succeed

My revision planner

1 Digital data

Representing data

Difference between information and data

- An information system *processes* **data** and produces information.
- Data consists of raw facts and figures with no meaning attached. When data is processed (or given meaning) it produces **information**.
- Therefore information is 'data with meaning'.

Product number	Product description
62351	8Tb hard drive

- 62351 can be considered as data as it is a sequence of digits. When we add meaning to this, such as 'Product number 62351 is an 8Tb hard drive', we provide information.

Storing data

- Computers store data in digital binary format.
- A Binary digIT (known as a **BIT**) has a value of 0 or 1.
- A nibble is represented by 4 bits.
- A character (such as a letter or a digit) is represented by 1 **byte** (or 8 bits).
- Multiples of bytes are referred to as:
  - 1 kilobyte (Kb) = 1024 bytes
  - 1 megabyte (Mb) = 1024 kilobytes
  - 1 gigabyte (Gb) = 1024 megabytes
  - 1 terabyte (Tb) = 1024 gigabytes
- These terms are used to describe computer memory capacity and the capacity of external storage devices.

Data Unprocessed facts or figures that, on their own, have no meaning

Information When data is entered into a computer system and is processed, it becomes information, or 'data with meaning'

Bit Has a value of 0 or 1 and is the smallest unit of computer storage

Byte 8 bits

Common mistake

Ensure you use the terms 'bit' and 'byte' correctly and do not mix them up.

Exam tip

Ensure you specify exactly how many bits are in a byte and how many bytes are in a Kb, Mb, Gb and Tb.

Data types

Data type	Description
Numeric	An integer number: • can be a positive or negative whole number • has no decimal or fractional parts. Real numbers: • include whole numbers (integers) and numbers with decimal/fractional parts • can be positive or negative.
Date/Time	Long date: displayed as Sunday, April 1, 2018. Medium date: displayed as dd-mmm-yyyy, e.g. 1-Apr-2018. Short date: displayed as dd/mm/yyyy, e.g. 01/04/2018. Long time: displayed as HH:MM:SS, e.g. 13:26:34 Medium time: displayed as HH:MM PM/AM, e.g. 01:26 PM Short time: displayed as HH:MM, e.g. 13:26

Data type	Description
Character/String	A character is a single letter or digit represented by the codes from the character set.
	ASCII is a character set based on each character being represented uniquely by a single byte.
	A string is textual data in the form of a sequence of characters.

Representing images

REVISED

- A **pixel** is the smallest unit of a digital image that can be displayed and edited.
  - Each pixel can have its own individual colour and is stored as a series of binary digits.
  - Combining pixels together will produce a complete image.
  - The quality of an image is referred to as 'image resolution'.
  - The greater the resolution, the greater the file size.
  - A typical JPEG image uses 24 bits to store a pixel.

> **Pixel** The smallest unit of a digital image that can be displayed and edited on a computer screen

Bitmap and vector-based graphics

Bitmap graphics	Vector-based graphics
• **Bitmap graphics** store details about every individual element (pixel) of the image. • Storing every pixel means the file size of a bitmap image can be very large. • A bitmap image can also be compressed, which reduces the file size.	• **Vector-based graphics** store information about the components that make up an image. • Components are based on mathematical objects such as lines, curves and shapes.

> **Bitmap graphics** Store details about every individual element (or pixel) that makes up an image
>
> **Vector-based graphics** Store information about the components that make up an image; these components are based on mathematical objects such as lines, curves and shapes

Common mistake

You need to ensure that you know the file formats for different types of graphics, such as still images and animated images.

Buffering and streaming a video

- **Streaming** allows a video to be viewed on a website without a time delay.
- Using streaming means the user can start watching the video as it downloads in 'real time'.
- A **buffer** is part of the memory used to store a downloaded part of the video before watching it.
- When the user is watching part of the video a buffer is used to download the next part of the video.
- Buffering helps prevent possible disruptions if there are time delays in streaming while the video is playing.

> **Streaming** Process that allows video to be viewed on a website straight away, without having to wait for the full video to be downloaded
>
> **Buffer** Computer memory used to store a part of the video download before it is watched

Representing sound

REVISED

Factor that affects sound quality	Description
Sample rate	Number of audio sound samples captured per second to represent the sounds digitally.
Bit depth	The number of bits used for each sound sample.
Bit rate	The quantity of data measured in bits that is processed in a given amount of time.

Analogue to digital conversion

- An analogue signal is a continuous varying signal that represents a physical quantity.
- Examples of analogue signals include sound waves and temperature.
- An analogue to digital converter (ADC) will sample a signal at regular time intervals.
- Samples are then converted to digital format.
- The frequency at which samples are taken is known as the sample rate, measured in Hertz (Hz).

Data portability

REVISED

- **Data portability** is the ability to transfer data from one computer to another or from one software application to another without having to re-enter the data.
- This is made possible by using a range of file formats.

Data portability
Transferring data from one computer to another or from one software application to another without having to re-enter the data

File format	Detail
JPEG	Joint Photographic Expert Group files support the compression of images.
TIFF	Tagged Image File Format files store bitmapped images.
PNG	Portable Network Graphics allow data compression of bitmapped graphics.
PICT	The standard file format for Apple graphics.
GIF	Graphics Interchange Format supports bitmapped image file format. Animated GIFs combine a series of GIF images and display them one after the other.
TXT	A plain text document that contains no text formatting.
CSV	A comma-separated value file is a text-format file used by database and spreadsheet applications.
RTF	Rich Text Format is used for text-based documents such as word processing.
MP3	A file format for compressing a sound.
MP4	Similar to MP3 but a file format that compresses both sound and video.
MIDI	Musical Instrument Digital Interface allows sound samples to be interchanged between different digital musical instruments.

File format	Detail
MPEG	Moving/Motion Picture Experts Group is a set of standards for compressing digital video.
AVI	Audio Video Interleaved is a multimedia file format.
PDF	Portable Document Format is a file format that is read only. The PDF file generated is usually smaller in file size than the original file.
WAV	Windows Audio Waveform is a file format standard for storing an audio bit stream on PCs.
WMA	Windows Media Audio is an audio data compression file format.

Data compression

- Websites require fast image and audio download speeds.
- Reducing the storage requirements of image files and audio files means faster upload and download speeds to and from the internet.
- **Data compression** is used to reduce file size and at the same time maintain the quality of the data contained in the file.
- There are two main types of data compression: lossy and lossless.

Lossy compression	Lossless compression
Lossy compression reduces the file size by removing some data, such as reducing the number of colours used in an image. This can result in a small reduction in the quality of an image. JPEG is an example of a lossy compression method.	Lossless compression maintains the quality of the file, therefore no data is lost. An example is WinZip, which reduces the file size for sending data over the internet and it can be recreated (unzipped) exactly as the file was before it was compressed.

> **Data compression** Used to convert digital data to as small a size as possible while still maintaining the quality of the data contained in the file; allows data to be sent over the internet with acceptable transmission speeds

> **Exam tip**
>
> Understand the difference between vector-based and bitmap graphics. Be familiar with why data is compressed and the range of file formats used.

Now test yourself

TESTED

1. How many bytes are there in 2 Mb? [2 marks]
2. Distinguish between data and information. [4 marks]
3. Name and describe three factors that affect the sound quality in a video. [6 marks]
4. Give two reasons why data is compressed. [4 marks]

> **Revision activity**
>
> - By referring to file sizes on a hard drive, calculate how many bytes are in each file.
> - Using the internet, find media that uses different file formats.
> - Compare buffering with streaming using an application such as Netflix.

2 Software

Application software and system software

Application software enables the computer to do a particular task, such as word processing.

System software:

- is the interface between computer hardware and user application programs
- enables the computer to operate its hardware and applications software
- includes the operating system and utility programs.

Function	Purpose
Allocating memory	Organises the use of main memory between programs and data files as they are transferred to and from the hard disc.
Storage	The operating system manages the storage of data and files on external devices, such as a hard drive.
Processing time	Allocates processing time between the programs that are currently in use by dividing the time into a number of *time slices* and, depending on the priority of the tasks to be processed, each task is allocated a number of these time slices.

Application software
Programs designed for an end user to do a particular task, such as word-processing and spreadsheet programs

System software Includes the operating system and all utility programs that enable the computer to operate its hardware and applications software

Modes of processing

Mode of processing	Description	Application
Real-time processing	<ul><li>Data is processed immediately after it is inputted.</li><li>Data files are updated before the next transaction takes place.</li><li>Output generated is processed quickly enough to influence the next input received.</li></ul>	Applications that use real-time processing include:<ul><li>airline/concert booking systems</li><li>online stock control systems.</li><li>air traffic control systems</li></ul>

Real-time processing
Processing of data occurs immediately data is input and updating occurs before the next input occurs

Batch processing Data is collected over a period of time, such as a day, and is processed together at a later time, such as overnight

Multi-user system The operating system switches between computers, giving each one a 'time slice'

Mode of processing	Description	Application
Batch processing	• Involves collecting groups of similar data over a period of time. • Data is input to a computer system at an off-peak time without any human involvement. • This type of processing suits applications where data does not have to be processed immediately.	Applications that make use of batch processing include: • billing systems (e.g. electricity/gas/telephone) • payroll systems (on a weekly or monthly basis) • banking systems (producing monthly customer statements).
Multi-user system	• Involves many users at different computers sharing the same processor. • Works by the operating system switching at high speed between the computers, giving each one in turn a small amount of processor time known as a 'time slice'.	Applications that make use of multi-user systems include multi-user database management systems.

> **Common mistake**
>
> Remember which applications use batch processing and which real-time processing; do not confuse the two.

Utility applications software

REVISED

A **utility application** is a program that carries out a specific task to assist the operating system, such as:

● **Disc defragmentation**:
  ○ rearranges the data stored on a hard disc so that files are stored in adjacent blocks
  ○ all the free blocks (free storage space) are together in the same part of the disk
  ○ speeds up the time it takes to access files because all the data is stored in the same area of the disk.
● Task scheduling:
  ○ processor time is divided amongst a number of tasks
  ○ uses time slices
  ○ implemented using a 'round robin' method.
● Data **backup** and restore:
  ○ a backup is a copy of the original data or file in case it gets damaged or lost
  ○ backup is used to restore the original data to its previous state by uploading the latest file onto the system
  ○ the procedure may involve backing up the complete data file (full backup) or just backing up the data that has changed (incremental backup).

> **Utility application** A program that performs a very specific task in managing system resources, such as a backup program
>
> **Disc defragmentation** Rearranges the data on a hard disc so that all the data is stored together and it becomes quicker to access the files
>
> **Backup** A second copy of a file made and stored on a different storage device in case the original file gets lost, or becomes corrupted or physically damaged

Role of anti-virus software

- Its main purpose is to detect, locate and remove a virus that can infect a computer system.
- A virus is a program that can attach itself to a file and then spread to other files.
- A virus can intentionally damage a computer system, prevent it from booting up or slow down the performance of a computer.
- **Anti-virus software** scans files stored on a computer and data entering a computer system, and compares these to a known database of viruses.
- The software can scan all storage devices connected to a computer, such as the internal hard drive, USB memory pens, and so on.

> **Anti-virus software**
> Software that scans files stored on a computer system, looking for a virus, and compares these to a known database of viruses; it can eliminate a virus

Exam tip

Ensure you don't reword a term when you are asked to define it. For example, if you are asked to define real-time processing, don't say that it is processing done in real time, but focus on the idea of updating the data as soon as a transaction takes place.

Now test yourself

TESTED

1 Identify three functions of system software. [3 marks]
2 Describe two features of anti-virus software. [4 marks]
3 Identify two applications that use batch processing. [2 marks]
4 Describe the main features of disc defragmentation and task scheduling as tasks carried out by utility software. [6 marks]

Revision activity

- Learn the main functions of system software.
- Be able to distinguish which applications use which of the different modes of processing.
- Review the different activities carried out by utility software.
- Understand the need for anti-virus software.

3 Database applications

Database concepts

- A **table** consists of a number of **records**.
- A record is represented as a row in a table.
- A **field** is part of a record that stores a single data item, represented by a column.
- A **key field** uniquely identifies one record.
- A **query** searches and filters data in a database that satisfies the query criteria.
- **Forms** are used to collect data to create a new record, modify an existing record or view records already stored in a table.
- **Reports** are used to present results from queries in an effective manner.
- Layout of reports can be customised, such as grouping similar data or presenting data in ascending or descending order.

> **Query** Used to search and extract data from a database to find the answer to a question
>
> **Form** Used to enter a new record, modify an existing record and view records already stored in a table
>
> **Report** Allows tables and results of queries to be presented in a user-friendly way

Activity Bookings

Location	BookingDate	ActivityDate	Activity	Surname	FirstName
Indoor					
	15-Sep-14	23-Mar-16	Archery	Turner	Ciaran
	07-Oct-14	30-Dec-15	Karting	Quinn	Michael
	12-Jun-13	16-Jun-15	Archery	McElhone	Liz
	14-Feb-14	16-Feb-16	Archery	Carroll	John
	10-Nov-13	13-Nov-15	Karting	McKelvey	Jude
	05-May-14	07-May-15	Archery	Stewart	Catherine
Outdoor					
	17-Mar-14	21-Mar-16	Quad Biking	Doherty	Ciara
	30-Mar-14	02-Apr-16	Horse Riding	Murray	Gareth
	17-Mar-14	20-Mar-16	Quad Biking	McNally	Mary

Report showing bookings made by customers grouped by location

Macros

- **Macros** are small programs that are written to perform a repetitive database task automatically.
- They are used to add functionality to forms and reports.
- Running a macro will result in instructions stored within the macro being executed with a single click of a button.

> **Macro** A small program written to perform a repetitive task automatically

Database relationships

- Database relationships link two or more tables in a database using a relationship type.
- For this to happen, a common field must be stored in each table; the key field from one table is stored in another table as a non-key field (also called a 'foreign key').
- Relationships are defined as one-to-one, one-to-many or many-to many.

Importing data

- It is possible to import a number of worksheets from a spreadsheet to a database package or vice versa.
- This gives organisations more flexibility in handling their data.

Data types

REVISED

Data type	Use
Text	Text and data that is a mixture of text and numbers, e.g. as a postcode
Number	Numeric data that requires a mathematical calculation
Date/Time	Dates and times
Currency	Monetary data; includes two decimal places
Autonumber	To create a key field, the computer generates sequential numbers that are automatically inserted for each new record created
Yes/No	Data that has two possible values, e.g. Yes/No or True/False; this is called a 'Boolean value'
OLE object	Object linking and embedding; objects created using a software package other than a database
Hyperlink	A link to web address (URL)
Attachment	A file attached to a record, e.g. a digital image
Calculated	The result of a calculation produced from another field in the record
Lookup wizard	A value can be selected from a predefined list and entered into the field

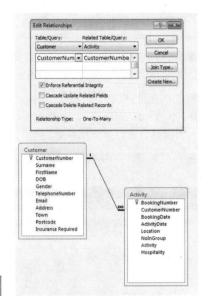

Here, referential integrity prevents the addition of a new record to the activity table that cannot be linked to a record in the customer table

Data type When a database is created, each field is allocated a data type; different data types are used for different fields, e.g. text or numeric; the data type defines the type of data associated with the field

Exam tip

There are several data types. You should be able to name each data type and suggest appropriate data types for fields.

Data validation

REVISED

- **Data validation** involves automatic checking of data at the input stage to ensure it is reasonable, sensible and within acceptable limits.
- It guarantees that data is present, and of the correct type, range or length.
- The computer checks data and either accepts the data, or rejects it and displays an error message.
- A number of data validation checks exist:

> **Data validation** Carried out by a computer automatically when data is input, it ensures that data is reasonable, sensible and within acceptable limits

Validation type	What is involved
Presence check	Ensures data is present; the field cannot be left blank
Length check	Ensures data is the correct number of characters
Type check	Ensures data is of the correct type, e.g. numeric/ text
Format check	Ensures data matches a predetermined pattern
Range check	Ensures data is within a lower and upper limit

Logical and comparison operators

REVISED

- Comparing a value against other data is a typical operation when data is queried in a database.
- Logical operators analyse two values and return either a true or a false result.
- Operators are denoted by the words AND, OR and BETWEEN.
- In the following example, the activity date must be between the two values stated for the result to be true.

<	Less than
<=	Less than or equal to
>	Greater than
>=	Greater than or equal to
=	Equal to
<>	Not equal to

Comparison operators

Field:	BookingDate	ActivityDate	Location	Activity	Surname	FirstName
Table:	Activity	Activity	Activity	Activity	Customer	Customer
Sort:						
Show:	☑	☑	☑	☑	☑	☑
Criteria:		Between #06/04/2015# And #05/04/2016#				
or:						

Here, the activity date must be between the two values shown if the result is to be true

Big data

- Big data refers to large amounts of data that have the potential to be mined for information.
- It can be described as the 3Vs: volume, variety and velocity.

Volume	<ul><li>Refers to the amount of data stored by organisations</li><li>Data is raw facts and figures that is unprocessed</li><li>Organisations now store large amounts of data from different sources, requiring large storage capacity hardware</li><li>Data storage is now measured in terabytes</li></ul>
Variety	<ul><li>Refers to the different types and varieties of data</li><li>Data is now stored in many formats, e.g. video and images; not just text</li><li>Data can be structured, semi-structured or unstructured</li></ul>
Velocity	<ul><li>Refers to the speed at which data can be processed</li><li>Due to large volumes of data, there is a need to use more powerful computers to process the data more quickly</li></ul>

Need for data analytics to interpret big data

- Data analytics involves analysing large volumes of data to produce useful information.
- This is beneficial to organisations for making decisions and planning for future growth.
- Specialised software such as data mining and statistical analysis are designed to process vast quantities of data.
- When data is in different formats (e.g. structured/unstructured) it makes preparing and processing the data more challenging for data analytics.

Exam tip

Ensure you are able to apply the skills you have learnt in practical assignments in an examination situation.

Now test yourself

TESTED

1 Complete the table below. [8 marks]

Field name	Data type	Validation check
Customer ID		
Date of birth		
Gender		
Email address		

2 Using the table above, identify and justify which field is suitable as a key field. [2 marks]
3 State three features that should be included in an on-screen form design. [3 marks]
4 Explain the difference between a query and a report, as used in a database. [4 marks]
5 Distinguish between volume, variety and velocity in the context of big data. [6 marks]

Revision activity

- Learn the main features of a database.
- Be able to evaluate the impact of big data on organisations.

4 Spreadsheet applications

Spreadsheet structure

- A spreadsheet contains one or more **worksheets**.
- A worksheet is presented as a grid in the form of rows and columns.
- Spreadsheets are designed to allow applications to perform calculations and recalculations automatically.
- Cells can store data in a variety of forms, for example text, number, date, **formula**, and so on.

> **Worksheet** A grid in the form of rows and columns; a spreadsheet is made up of a number of worksheets, and each worksheet can be given a different name as a reference point
>
> **Formula** A mathematical equation or an expression that is used to define how a particular cell is linked to other cells in a worksheet

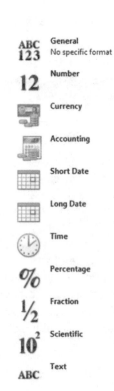

A cell reference is a column value first and then a row value C5.

A block of cells G4:G12.

Each worksheet is a separate tab.

- Spreadsheet data can be formatted as: general, number, currency, date, time, percentage, and so on.
- Formatting can also control the appearance of a cell, for example aligning text, changing the font or adding a border or background colour.
- Conditional formatting allows cell shading or font colour to be applied to a cell or group of cells if a specified condition is met.
- A value inputted to a given cell(s) can be controlled using a data validation.

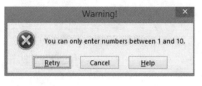

ABC 123	General — No specific format
12	Number
	Currency
	Accounting
	Short Date
	Long Date
	Time
%	Percentage
1/2	Fraction
10^2	Scientific
ABC	Text

Worheet presentation

Templates

- A **template** refers to a document that has been preformatted using a predetermined layout for the user.
- It serves as a starting point for a new document.
- For example, a budget template will have allocated places for entering data such as income and expenditure for a company budget.

> **Template** A predefined layout containing the main elements of the document it represents; the contents and layout of the template can be edited to suit the needs of the specific user

Importing data

- Data can be **imported** into a spreadsheet from other software sources, for example a database table.
- In some cases, the file being imported may have to be in a certain format, for example CSV (comma-separated value), before the import process can begin.

> **Importing data** Allows data produced in another software application, such as data from a database package, to be used in a spreadsheet

Headers and footers

- To improve the presentation of worksheets, headers (placed at the top of the worksheet) and footers (placed at the bottom of the worksheet) can be added.
- These can be used to add page numbers, filenames or dates.

Formulas and functions

- Formulas and **functions** allow a spreadsheet to perform calculations and automatic re-calculations.
- When a formula or function is entered into a cell it can be replicated quickly down a column or across a row using the 'Fill' function.
- The table below gives examples of simple functions.

> **Function** Part of the software application that performs a specific task and returns a value, such as finding the average of a list of numbers

Function	Example	Meaning
SUM	=SUM(C3:C10)	The cells in the range C3 to C10 are added together and the total displayed.
AVERAGE	=AVERAGE(C3:C10)	The cells in the range C3 to C10 are added together and the average calculated.
MAX	=MAX(C3:C10)	The highest value in the cell range C3 to C10 is returned.
MIN	=MIN(C3:C10)	The lowest value in the cell range C3 to C10 is returned.

Using the IF statement

- This statement will examine a condition, resulting in one of two actions being carried out.

```
IF <condition is true>
    THEN
            <action 1 is carried out>
    ELSE
            <action 2 is carried out>
ENDIF
```

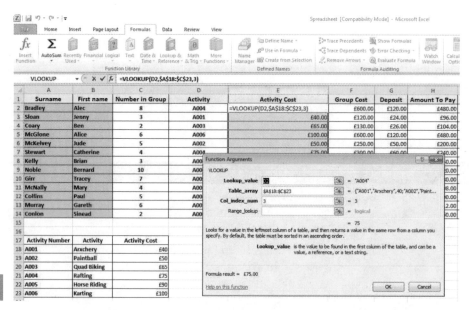

	A	B	C	D	E	F	G	H
1	Surname	First name	Number in Group	Activity Cost	Group Cost	Deposit	Amount To Pay	Next Booking Discount
2	Bradley	Alec	8	£54.50	£436.00	£87.20	£348.80	=IF(E2<=150,"10%","20%")
3	Sloan	Jenny	3	£26.00	£78.00	£15.60	£62.40	10%
4	Coary	Ben	2	£45.50	£91.00	£18.20	£72.80	10%
5	McGlone	Alice	6	£52.00	£312.00	£62.40	£249.60	20%
6	McKelvey	Jude	5	£34.00	£170.00	£34.00	£136.00	20%
7	Stewart	Catherine	4	£45.50	£182.00	£36.40	£145.60	20%
8	Kelly	Brian						10%
9	Noble	Bernard						20%
10	Girr	Tracey						20%
11	McNally	Mary						10%
12	Collins	Paul						20%
13	Murray	Gareth						20%
14	Conlon	Sinead						10%

Function Arguments

IF

Logical_test E2<=150 = FALSE
Value_if_true "10%" = "10%"
Value_if_false "20%" = "20%"

= "20%"

Checks whether a condition is met, and returns one value if TRUE, and another value if FALSE.

Value_if_false is the value that is returned if Logical_test is FALSE. If omitted, FALSE is returned.

Formula result = 20%

Help on this function   OK   Cancel

Spreadsheet showing the IF statement function

Using the VLookup function

- This function uses the value in a selected cell to 'lookup' a match in a column of a lookup table (vertical lookup).
- It returns a value from a specified column from the same row of the lookup table.

Spreadsheet [Compatibility Mode] - Microsoft Excel

File   Home   Insert   Page Layout   Formulas   Data   Review   View

VLOOKUP   ▾ (X ✓ fx =VLOOKUP(D2,$A$18:$C$23,3)

	A	B	C	D	E	F	G	H
1	Surname	First name	Number in Group	Activity	Activity Cost	Group Cost	Deposit	Amount To Pay
2	Bradley	Alec	8	A004	=VLOOKUP(D2,$A$18:$C$23,3)	£600.00	£120.00	£480.00
3	Sloan	Jenny	3	A001	£40.00	£120.00	£24.00	£96.00
4	Coary	Ben	2	A003	£65.00	£130.00	£26.00	£104.00
5	McGlone	Alice	6	A006	£100.00	£600.00	£120.00	£480.00
6	McKelvey	Jude	5	A002	£50.00	£250.00	£50.00	£200.00
7	Stewart	Catherine	4	A004	£75.00	£300.00	£60.00	£240.00
8	Kelly	Brian	3	A00				0.00
9	Noble	Bernard	10	A00				0.00
10	Girr	Tracey	7	A00				0.00
11	McNally	Mary	4	A00				8.00
12	Collins	Paul	5	A00				0.00
13	Murray	Gareth	6	A00				2.00
14	Conlon	Sinead	2	A00				0.00
15								
16								
17	Activity Number	Activity	Activity Cost					
18	A001	Arxchery	£40					
19	A002	Paintball	£50					
20	A003	Quad Biking	£65					
21	A004	Rafting	£75					
22	A005	Horse Riding	£90					
23	A006	Karting	£100					

Function Arguments

VLOOKUP

Lookup_value 33 = "A004"
Table_array $A$18:$C$23 = {"A001","Arxchery",40;"A002","Paint...
Col_index_num 3 = 3
Range_lookup = logical

= 75

Looks for a value in the leftmost column of a table, and then returns a value in the same row from a column you specify. By default, the table must be sorted in an ascending order.

Lookup_value is the value to be found in the first column of the table, and can be a value, a reference, or a text string.

Formula result = £75.00

Help on this function   OK   Cancel

Lookup table

Now test yourself answers and glossary at www.hoddereducation.co.uk/myrevisionnotes

Relative and absolute cell references

- When a formula is automatically copied down a column or across a row using the 'Fill' function, a **relative cell reference** adjusts and changes the formulas to make sure it refers to the correct cell(s), for example when 'filled down', the formula =C2*D2 changes to =C3*D3 and then to =C4*D4, and so on.

	A	B	C	D	E
1	Surname	First name	Number in Group	Activity Cost	Group Cost
2	Bradley	Alec	8	£54.50	=C2*D2
3	Sloan	Jenny	3	£26.00	=C3*D3

- In some cases, the cell reference must remain the same when it is copied. This is called an **absolute cell reference**, for example if converting an amount to pay from pounds into Euros the same exchange rates are required for each calculation.

Relative cell reference
Changes a formula's cell references to refer to the next cell(s) when the formula is copied down a column or across a row

Absolute cell reference
When a formula is copied to other cells, part of the cell reference does not change as the formula is modified

Common mistake

Ensure you reference cells correctly, such as A2 rather than 2A.

Using charts to display results

- Using charts can greatly assist in the communication of information when an organisation is doing a presentation for its clients.
- A range of charts can be used, such as bar charts, pie charts, and so on.

Using macros in spreadsheets

- When using a spreadsheet, a **macro** can eliminate the need for the user to repeat the steps of commonly performed tasks over and over again.
- Tasks could range from adding a date to a worksheet to sophisticated calculations that require complex formulas

Macro A small program written to perform a repetitive task automatically

Using spreadsheets for data modelling

- Spreadsheets are used in organisations for **data modelling**.
- The model is controlled by a set of rules defined by formulas. By changing the formulas, the rules of the model can be varied.
- Being able to answer 'what if' questions, such as 'What if we increase the number of employees by 10 per cent; will it decrease our profits?', allow businesses to predict future outcomes.
- Using a spreadsheet to model data can assist in making better-informed decisions.

> **Data modelling** Uses mathematical formulas and calculations on data to help predict outcomes for given situations

Exam tip

There are several data formats – you should be able to name each format and suggest suitable data types for each cell.

Be able to use the correct notation when asked to suggest a suitable formula or function for a given cell.

Revision activity

- Learn the main features of a spreadsheet.
- Be able to explain how each function can be used.
- Select row and column ranges from a worksheet to create a graph.
- Use examples to illustrate how a spreadsheet could be used for data modelling.

Common mistake

Ensure correct use of notation for functions.

John is planning a special party celebration for his mother.

	A	B	C	D	E
1	Party venue	Club 2020			
2	Available money	£400.00			
3	Party costing				
4	Item	Estimated Cost	Actual Cost	Difference	Over Budget
5	Hire of venue	£100.00	£110.00	-£10.00	Yes
6	DJ	£120.00	£100.00	£20.00	No
7	Food	£60.00	£75.00	-£15.00	Yes
8	Prizes	£50.00	£70.00	-£20.00	Yes
9	Decorations	£50.00	£45.00	£5.00	No
10	Tickets	£25.00	£30.00	-£5.00	Yes
11	Insurance	£35.00	£30.00	£5.00	No
12	Other	£60.00	£90.00	-£30.00	Yes
13	Total Costs	£500.00	£550.00	-£50.00	
14	Over Budget	£150.00			

1 How have the cells in row 3 been formatted? [2 marks]
2 How can the data in cells B5 to B12 be used to help John plan the party? [2 marks]
3 Copy and complete the table below to show the formula used to calculate the values in the following cells. [3 marks]

Cell	Formula
D5	
B13	
B14	

4 John's spending does not match his available money. What information is available to him in column E? [2 marks]
5 Copy and complete the IF statement that provides the information in E11.
   =IF(_____<_____,"Yes","No") [2 marks]
6 John wants to show the information about party costs on a graph. By making reference to cells, explain how a bar graph could be produced. [3 marks]
7 Explain an advantage of presenting information on a graph. [2 marks]
8 John wants to create a macro to print the graph. What is a macro? [2 marks]

5 Computer hardware

Central processing unit (CPU)

- The **CPU** (central processing unit) is often referred to as the 'brain' of the computer.
- Its main role is to process programs and data.
- It does this by repeatedly fetching an instruction from memory and executing it (**fetch–execute cycle**).

Component	Role
Control unit	<ul><li>Decides which instruction to carry out next</li><li>Fetches it from memory</li><li>Decodes the instruction and executes (or obeys) the instruction</li><li>Repeats the process (fetch–execute cycle)</li></ul>
Arithmetic and logic unit (ALU)	<ul><li>Carries out arithmetic calculations, e.g. addition, multiplication, subtraction, division</li><li>Performs logical comparisons to assist with decision-making by using the operators AND, OR and NOT</li></ul>
Immediate access store (IAS)	<ul><li>Stores all programs and data temporarily while they are in use</li><li>During the fetch–execute cycle, instructions are fetched from their specific storage location in the IAS using an address</li><li>Each memory location has a unique address assigned to it</li></ul>

> **CPU** Central processing unit; the processor or 'brains' of the computer. This is where data is processed and calculations take place
>
> **Fetch–execute cycle** A computer process that locates a program instruction from internal memory, decodes the instruction and carries out the action required; this process is then repeated for the rest of the program instructions

Fetch–execute cycle

- The CPU includes a number of registers.
- These are high-speed memory locations, each used for specific purposes.
- The registers below have an important role during the fetch-execute cycle.

Register	Purpose during fetch–execute cycle
Program counter (PC)	A PC stores the address (memory location reference) of the next instruction to be fetched. It is automatically incremented by 1 every time an instruction is fetched.
Memory address register (MAR)	The address of the current instruction or data being executed is temporarily stored in the MAR.

Register	Purpose during fetch–execute cycle
Memory data register (MDR)	This register will temporarily store data being fetched from or written to the main memory of the CPU.
Instruction register (IR)	This register temporarily stores the current instruction to de decoded and then executed.
Accumulator	When calculations take place on data, the results are initially stored in the accumulator before being transferred and stored in the main memory.

Factors that influence the speed of processing

REVISED ▢

Clock speed

- The clock speed measures the number of instruction cycles the CPU can deal with in a second.
- The standard unit of measurement for clock speed is gigahertz (GHz).

Cache

- Cache temporarily stores frequently used instructions and data.
- It is quicker to search cache memory than RAM, thus increasing processor speed.

Processor core

- A core can be defined as a single processor.
- More advanced CPUs contain more than one core, which will increase their ability to run many programs at the same time, for example, a 'quad core' processor has four processors.

Computer hardware devices

REVISED ▢

Device	Purpose	Advantages	Disadvantages
Microphone	• Accepts sound input or human voice into a computer system • A *voice recognition system* can convert sound to text	• Faster to speak using a microphone than typing words using a keyboard • It is hands free, allowing users to carry out other activities at the same time as voice input	• The recognition rate of spoken words can be low if there is background noise • Sound files require greater storage capacity than text files
Mouse	• Used to control the pointer/cursor on a VDU • Uses built-in sensors to detect movements and send corresponding signals back to the computer • Also includes buttons used to make selections on the screen	• Easy to use and requires little or no training • Quicker to select menus and icons compared to using a keyboard	• Experienced users find it slow compared to using 'hot keys' • Need a flat surface (additional space) to function properly

Device	Purpose	Advantages	Disadvantages
Graphics digitiser	• Allows a user to hand-draw images, which are captured by the computer • Consists of a flat electronic sensitive surface and a stylus pen	• More natural to draw diagrams with a stylus than with a mouse • Using a stylus produces more accurate and detailed drawings	• Not suitable for selecting menus and pointing at menu items • More expensive than a mouse
Touchscreen	• Looks similar to ordinary computer screens, with a touch-sensitive surface/membrane • When the screen is touched the position is calculated as a (x,y) co-ordinate	• User does not require much ICT competence compared to using a keyboard • Users can select and enter options much faster than using a keyboard	• Limited number of options are available on screen • Screens can become dirty quickly
Speaker	• Allows sound to be outputted • May be internal or external speaker • In addition to the hardware, a sound card needs to be fitted inside the computer	• Useful for visually impaired users: text or figures can be spoken by the computer • Natural way to communicate with users	• External speakers require additional desk space compared to using headphones • Speakers can distract other users in the same office who are doing other tasks
Laser printer	• A laser beam is used to scan the image of the page to be printed onto a drum by building a pattern of static electricity • This attracts toners (printer ink) to reproduce the page	• Faster to print in bulk compared to an ink jet printer • Produces high-quality text and graphic output	• Colour laser printers are expensive to purchase and use • Because they are non-impact printers, multipart stationery cannot be used
3D printer	• Gradually prints a solid 3D object one layer at a time	• Time taken to produce an object is much faster than using conventional methods • Can print on a variety of surfaces, e.g. plastic, metal, ceramic	• Limited form of printing as it can only print a prototype (not full scale) • Not economical for large-scale manufacturing
Hard disc drive	• Consists of a number of rigid discs stacked on a spindle and enclosed in a sealed unit • Formatting a disc divides the surface into a number of tracks and sectors • As the discs rotate at high speeds the read/write heads move back and forth across the surface	• The cost per gigabyte is cheaper than other forms of external storage • Storage capacity is much greater compared to solid-state storage devices	• Due to moving parts, such as read/write heads, they are prone to breaking down • Access speeds are slower than 'flash' memory devices

Exam tip

When you are asked about the features of a hardware device you can use advantages and disadvantages, as these are also features. When answering a question about an advantage or disadvantage, it would be better if you could compare it to another device.

Now test yourself answers and glossary at www.hoddereducation.co.uk/myrevisionnotes

High-definition (HD) storage media

- HD storage media use laser technology to store and retrieve data at high data transfer speeds to and from optical discs.
- They can store over 50 Gb of data (more than ten times the amount that can be stored on a DVD).
- Instead of a red laser (used on a DVD) they use a blue laser, which burns much smaller pits onto the surface.
- This increases the density and therefore the storage capacity.

Solid-state storage devices

- A solid-state storage device is referred to as 'flash memory' and non-volatile.
- USB memory sticks are a type of solid-state storage.
- They are compact, portable, have a large storage capacity and do not require a software driver to be installed (and so are described as 'plug and play' devices).

Memory cards

- These are electronic flash memory storage devices.
- They are used in a range of digital devices, including mobile phones, digital cameras and MP4 players.
- For example, in mobile phones a SIM (subscriber identity module) card is used to store data.

Smart cards

- Bank cards use a form of flash memory known as 'chip and PIN'.
- Cards contain a small embedded integrated circuit (IC), which allows data to be written to and read from the card using a smart card reader.

Internal memory

REVISED

RAM (random access memory)	<ul><li>Memory can be read from or written to (volatile)</li><li>Stores programs and data that the user is currently using, e.g. parts of the operating system, applications software such as Word and documents being edited</li><li>The size of RAM can influence the speed of the processor (the larger the RAM capacity the faster the processor)</li></ul>
ROM (read only memory)	<ul><li>Memory can be read from but not written to (non-volatile)</li><li>Used to store programs that the computer frequently requires, e.g. the booting-up program for Windows that runs automatically when the computer is switched on</li></ul>

Common mistakes

- Do not mix up ROM and RAM with volatile and non-volatile.
- Ensure you avoid answering questions with non-technical language such as 'is faster', 'is quicker', and so on.

Now test yourself

1 Name three components of the CPU. [3 marks]
2 Describe the purpose of two registers used in the fetch–execute cycle. [4 marks]
3 Distinguish between clock speed and processor core with reference to processing speeds. [4 marks]
4 Compare RAM and ROM as two forms of internal memory. [4 marks]
5 State two advantages of using a touchscreen as an input device. [4 marks]
6 State two disadvantages of using a microphone to input data to a computer system. [4 marks]

Revision activity

- Learn the main features of the CPU components.
- Be able to briefly explain the fetch–execute cycle by referring to registers.
- Be able to state two advantages and two disadvantages for each hardware device.

6 Network technologies

Computer networks – LAN and WAN

- A network consists of a number of computers linked together by using either cable or wireless technology.
- A LAN (**local area network**) is spread over a small geographical area, such as a building.
- A WAN (**wide area network**) is spread over a large geographical area on a global scale and requires a telecommunications link to all computers on the network to communicate.

World Wide Web, internet and intranet

- The World Wide Web is an application that uses the internet.
- The internet is an example of a wide area network (WAN).
- A website has a unique address, known as its URL (**uniform resource locator**).
- Each website consists of a number of webpages developed using a web authoring language such as HTML (**hypertext markup language**).
- Web pages are interconnected using hyperlinks, and the first page is called the 'home page'.
- To allow websites to be accessed using the internet, they require a communications protocol known as http (**hypertext transfer protocol**).
- An intranet is similar to the internet, but is managed by an organisation and only authorised users, with a username and password, can access the content.
- The 'internet of things' (IoT) describes the impact of the internet on how we live and work.
- Any device that can communicate using **Wi-Fi** technology is included in the internet of things.

> **Local area network** A network where computers are geographically close together, e.g. in the same building
>
> **Wide area network** A network where computers are geographically far apart, e.g. in different cities, and are connected by telephone lines and/or radio waves

> **Exam tip**
>
> Understand the difference between LAN and WAN.

> **Uniform resource locator** The address that can be entered into the address bar to locate a website
>
> **Hypertext markup language** The language used to define the structure of webpages; it is often combined with CSS and JavaScript to create hypermedia applications presented to users via browser software for the World Wide Web

Network communications technology

Wi-Fi (Wireless Fidelity)	• Wi-Fi connections use radio waves and a wireless router • Devices with a built-in wireless adapter can connect to a Wi-Fi network • Advantage of using a Wi-Fi network is that there is no need for cabling • Disadvantage is the limited distance on how far the signal can travel and variations on the signal strength depending on proximity to the wireless router
Bluetooth	• Uses short-range wireless technology to connect two devices together • For the devices to begin transferring data between each other they have to be synchronised or 'paired' • Since the devices communicate directly with each other there is no need to have a router

Optical fibre	• Consists of a bundle of glass strands; each strand carries one data signal, which means many data signals can be sent at one time in the bundle • Data is transmitted as pulses of light • Advantage of using glass is that signals (or data) cannot be interfered – it is very secure • Disadvantage is it requires the use of repeaters for data to travel over large distances
Mobile communication technology	• 4G mobile-phone technology is capable of high-speed data access and high-quality video streaming using wireless technology on a global scale • 5G mobile-phone technology is more reliable and has greater speeds than 4G • It fully supports wireless World Wide Web with little or no limitations, e.g. users can watch television programmes on their mobile phones in HD format

Hypertext transfer protocol A protocol used by the World Wide Web that defines how messages are formatted and transmitted by web servers

Wi-Fi A wireless medium that allows devices to connect and communicate using radio waves

Router A hardware device that connects a number of networks together by either cable or wireless, to allow for data transmission

Bluetooth A short-range wireless technology that allows two devices to connect for the purpose of communication

Optical fibre A technology that uses very thin glass strands to send data at very fast transmission speeds

Network resources

REVISED

Network interface card (NIC)

- A **NIC** is an electronic circuit board built into a computer to allow it to be connected to a network.
- It allows each computer to communicate with the **file server** and the other computers on the network.
- It has a 'port' to allow a network cable (such as Ethernet) to be attached.
- Portable computers such as laptops are supplied with a standard wireless network interface card (WNIC).

Network cables

- A network cable physically connects a computer to a network.
- Generally, cables are made of copper and the data travels along the cables to and from the file server.

Switch

- A **switch** allows a large number of computers on a network to be connected.
- It checks the destination of data it receives and ensures it is forwarded to the intended computer.

Router

- This is a hardware device that connects a number of networks together by either cable or wireless.
- It examines data as it passes, and forwards the data using the most appropriate route to its destination.
- IP addresses are used to determine the route the data travels on.

Network interface card An electronic board fitted to a computer to allow it to be connected to a network

File server A powerful computer on a network, the main purpose of which is to store users' files

Switch A hardware device that allows a computer to connect to it using a cable to access a network

Common mistake

Learn the differences between a router and a switch, and avoid confusing the two.

Network topologies

Bus network

- In this network, computers are connected to a main cable known as a 'backbone'.
- Data can travel in both directions along the backbone.
- To add a new computer to a bus network its cable is attached to the backbone.

Star network

- Computers are connected by their own cable to a file server.
- All data on the network must pass through the file server.
- An additional computer can be added by attaching it (using its own cable) to the file server.

Ring network

- Each computer is directly connected to two other adjacent computers to form a ring.
- All data travels in one direction by visiting each computer in turn until it reaches its intended destination.
- To add a new computer to the network the cable between two existing computers has to be broken and each part of the broken cable attached to the new computer.

Common mistakes

Learn the features of ring, star and bus topologies and avoid mixing them up.

Virus A program that is designed to damage a computer system

Advantages and disadvantages of networking

Advantages	Disadvantages
• Users can save their work on the file server and retrieve it on any other computer within the network. • Expensive hardware devices, e.g. laser printers, can be shared by all computers on the network. • Installing software and updates once onto the file server allows all computers to access software quickly.	• A software **virus** can quickly spread across the network, affecting all user data and the software. • When a large number of users are logged onto the network, access speeds can be slow. • The set-up costs can be expensive as additional hardware, e.g. file servers, network interface cards, switches and routers, has to be purchased.

Exam tip

When asked about the features of a network topology, use another topology to cross reference.

Revision activity

- Understand the features of the WWW.
- Be able to describe the communications technology used on networks.
- Learn definitions of network resources.
- Be able to compare network topologies used on a LAN.
- Learn two advantages and two disadvantages of a network.

Now test yourself

TESTED

1 Distinguish between a LAN and a WAN. [2 marks]
2 State two features of Wi-Fi technology. [2 marks]
3 Name and describe three network resources. [9 marks]
4 Describe the main features of a bus network. [6 marks]
5 State two advantages and two disadvantages of using networks. [4 marks]

7 Cyberspace, network security and data transfer

Cyber crime and threats to cyber security

REVISED

- **Cyber crime** is defined as using a computer to commit a crime.

Threat	Example of threat to cyber security
Hacking	Gaining unauthorised access to a computer with the intention of corrupting or stealing data stored on a hard drive
Pornography	Often used as a means of hiding **malware**; when an employee downloads adult content they are increasing the risk of business data being corrupted by a virus or stolen by an unauthorised user
Cyber stalking	Individuals using technology to harass others, e.g. sending inappropriate emails or making inappropriate comments on social media
Data theft	Theft of personal data, which are then used to commit identify fraud, e.g. passport applications
Denial of service	A malicious attack on a network, e.g. preventing users from logging on to access their data or email accounts
Digital forgery	Intentionally and falsely altering digital content, e.g. changing a passport photograph and/or names to sell on to criminals
Cypher defamation	Using the internet to intentionally damage the reputation of a person or organisation
Spamming	Sending 'junk' emails, e.g. adverts for products; as a result, the inbox becomes overloaded and time is wasted opening and reading such emails
Phishing	Sending emails that appear to be from a reliable source; these emails often ask the recipient to update their personal information by clicking a hyperlink that opens up a web page – this information is then used by hackers for the purpose of identity theft

Cyber crime Using a computer to intentionally commit a crime, e.g. stealing data or money

Hacking Gaining unauthorised access to a computer with the intention of corrupting or stealing data

Malware Malicious software that is unintentionally downloaded onto a computer by a user

Spamming Sending 'junk' emails to users, for example adverts for products

Phishing Sending emails that, when opened, appear to be from a reliable source asking the user to update their personal information. This information is then used by hackers for the purpose of identity theft

Malware

REVISED

- Malware is malicious software that is downloaded onto a computer unintentionally by using the internet or from email attachments.

Form of malware	Outcome
Virus	• Can enter the network through browsing the internet, opening email attachments, via a USB storage device, etc. • Can store itself automatically on a computer hard drive as a hidden file • Can be activated when a certain program is opened or when a predetermined condition is met, e.g. a certain date

Common mistake

When answering questions on viruses, don't use loose language such as 'it destroys a computer', as this is not true.

30   Now test yourself answers and glossary at www.hoddereducation.co.uk/myrevisionnotes

Form of malware	Outcome
Trojan horse	• Gains entry to a user's computer 'in disguise' • Tricks the user by encouraging them to open and download a software program that they require • Once installed, some Trojans can do serious damage, e.g. deleting data files
Worm	• Spreads around a computer system by replicating itself • Spreads around a network without the need to be attached to any document or program • Requires bandwidth, which can result in slower data transmission speeds
Key logger	• A program that is designed to record keyboard activities performed by users (known as 'keystrokes') • The keystrokes are saved as a log file and then sent to the person who created the program • The main purpose is to steal personal information from users, e.g. bank details
Spyware	• Software that is secretly installed on a user's computer from the internet • Tracks user activities, gathering useful information, e.g. credit card and password details when used on websites

Exam tips

- When referring to cyber crime, be able to explain threats by using examples.
- Be able to refer to different types of virus when describing malware.

Network protection

REVISED

Data encryption

- **Encryption** uses special software to encode or 'scramble' data before it is transmitted.
- This makes the data unreadable or meaningless if intercepted.
- Users with the encryption key software can unscramble the data when it arrives at its destination.

Data encryption The process of scrambling data using a 'key' before it is transmitted onto a network

Usernames and passwords

- Users on a network are allocated a unique user ID and a randomly generated password.
- Users are required to change passwords regularly by the network software to enhance security.
- Each time a user logs on, the system checks their user ID and password against a database of user details.
- Network software can disable the user ID for a period of time after unsuccessful log-on attempts.

Access levels

- Users are allocated different levels of access to files.
- Access rights can be classified as 'read only', 'read and copy' or 'read and write'.
- Access rights are stored in a table linked to the user ID and password.

Backup

- If data is lost or becomes corrupted, the network should have a method of recovering the data.
- A file **backup** ensures that a copy of the data can be loaded or restored on to the system if the original data is lost or corrupted.
- Network backups are usually automatically scheduled to run at certain times, e.g. the end of each day.

> **Backup** A second copy of a file made and stored on a different storage device in case the original file gets lost, or becomes corrupted or physically damaged

Firewall

- **Firewalls** monitor and filter data entering or leaving a network.
- They use security settings to block data that does not comply with the organisation's rules.

> **Firewall** A piece of software or hardware that is used to monitor and filter data that enters or leaves a network

Common mistakes

Make sure you refer to a firewall in terms of monitoring data that both enters and leaves a network (not just enters a network!).

Protocols used for data transfer

REVISED

- Communication **protocols** are agreed standards or rules for sending or receiving data on a network.
- Protocols are agreed by hardware manufacturers and software developers.

> **Protocol** A set of rules to allow for communication between two different computer systems

File transport protocol (FTP)	• Protocol that allows users to download or upload files over the internet • To ensure that data is sent in a secure way, data encryption is used
Hypertext transfer protocol (http)	• A protocol used by the WWW to transfer webpages over the internet • Sends a command on behalf of the user to the web server to request a webpage • If a webpage cannot be located the http will report an error, e.g. '404 File Not Found'
Hypertext transfer protocol secure (https)	• Uses a secure socket layer (SSL) to ensure data is transmitted securely over the internet • Uses encryption for sending data and decryption for receiving data • Web browsers display a padlock icon on screen to show that the web page currently in use is secure • The main use of this protocol is in financial applications, e.g. online PayPal transactions

> **File transport protocol** A protocol that allows users to upload and download files from file servers using the internet
>
> **Hypertext transfer protocol** A protocol used by the World Wide Web that defines how messages are formatted and transmitted by web servers
>
> **Hypertext transfer protocol secure** A protocol used by the World Wide Web for transmitting messages securely using data encryption

Revision activity

- Learn four different threats to cybersecurity.
- Learn four different forms of malware.
- Understand the different methods used to protect networks.
- Distinguish between http and https.

Now test yourself

TESTED

1 Name and describe two threats to cyber security. [6 marks]
2 Identify three different levels of access. [3 marks]
3 Explain how data encryption is used when transferring files across a network. [4 marks]
4 Compare the following internet protocols: http and https. [6 marks]

8 Cloud computing

What is cloud computing?

- 'The **cloud**' refers to a number of resources, such as data storage and software applications, that are offered and delivered on demand to an organisation using the internet.
- This means organisations access their data and programs over the internet instead of accessing their own hard drive(s) locally.

> **Cloud** Resources and storage hosted online; the cloud can be accessed on a global scale using any device that can connect to the internet

Advantages of cloud computing

- Cost effective: the cost of providing software, maintenance and upgrades is cheaper than buying software licences for multiple users.
- Unlimited storage: there is a limit to the storage capacity when an organisation only uses their hard drives. In the cloud, there is unlimited storage capacity available.
- Software updates: automatic software updates are available, therefore there is no need for an organisation to spend time installing new software updates.
- **Backup** and recovery: data is backed up automatically at regular intervals, therefore there is no need for an organisation to have procedures in place for backing up data and recovering data in the event of a disaster.
- Greater accessibility to information: employees of an organisation can access their data anywhere, and from any device, as long as they have an internet connection.
- Reduction in carbon footprint: less technology is needed thus reducing the demand for electricity and a reduction in the organisation's carbon footprint.

> **File backup** A physical copy of a file stored in a secure location in case the original file gets lost, destroyed or corrupted

Disadvantages of cloud computing

- **Bandwidth** limitations: cloud providers may only offer a limited bandwidth allowance and impose additional charges for greater bandwidth.
- Potential downtime: cloud computing is reliant on the internet. If the connection or a device, such as a router, fails then there is no access to the organisation's resources.
- Security: data can be at risk from hackers when using the internet.

> **Bandwidth** The amount of data that can be transmitted over a network in a fixed amount of time, measured in bits per second

Impact of cloud computing on gaming

- Game developers are able to reduce their costs as they don't need to pay high street shops to sell their games.
- Since the internet is global, game producers have the advantage of access to a much larger global customer base using the cloud, leading to increased sales and higher profits.
- Customers normally pay less for a game, as it can be purchased online.
- When a game is purchased it can be downloaded immediately.
- Using the cloud means that gamers do not need to continually purchase more up-to-date hardware as they have access to powerful game servers and game **streaming** using the internet.
- The cloud can support more complex visual effects, which are a feature of modern games, and provide additional storage for gamers.
- A drawback for the user is the possible limited broadband capacity that is not capable of streaming high quality.

> **Streaming** Process that allows video to be viewed on a website straight away, without having to wait for the full video to be downloaded

Impact of cloud computing on file storage

- Cloud-based systems have a facility to store large data files on very powerful high-capacity cloud servers.
- Automatic saving of data files to the cloud takes place every few seconds, reducing the chance of losing data.
- Cloud providers ensure that data files are stored permanently online.

Impact of cloud computing on file sharing

- Cloud technology allows users to collaborate and share files from anywhere in the world.
- Users can upload files to the cloud and share these with other users.
- The cloud allows employees from different parts of the world to collaborate as a team on the same project.
- Synchronisation means that when a user makes a change to a file this change will appear in the versions used by others.
- Google Docs is an example of file-sharing using the cloud.

> **Exam tip**
>
> Understand the impact on the areas named in this section (as they are stated in the specification), as they can appear in the examination.

Now test yourself

TESTED

1 Define the term 'cloud computing'. [2 marks]
2 State two advantages to an organisation of using cloud computing. [3 marks]
3 Describe two disadvantages of cloud computing to an organisation. [4 marks]
4 Evaluate the impact of cloud computing on gaming. [6 marks]

> **Revision activity**
>
> - Learn three advantages and three disadvantages of cloud computing.
> - Be able to describe the impact of the cloud on gaming
> - Be able to describe the impact of the cloud on file storage
> - Be able to describe the impact of the cloud on file sharing

9 Ethical, legal and environmental impact of digital technology on wider society

Legislation relevant to digital technology

- The government is responsible for creating and updating laws to encourage the appropriate use of computers, digital information and software in today's society.

Consumer Contracts Regulations 2013

- Consumer Contracts Regulations state the rights of customers when shopping online.
- Online traders must provide customers with full descriptions of products being sold.
- All costs must be made available, such as product prices and delivery and return charges.
- A customer has the right to cancel an order, and be given a full refund, for physical products (up to 14 days from the date received).
- Customers who purchase downloaded products containing digital content are not entitled to cancel their order.
- Products sold online that include digital content must contain details on hardware and software compatibility.

Data Protection Act 1998

- Personal data is stored on a wide range of computers owned by different organisations.
- The Data Protection Act controls how this personal information can be used by organisations.
- This legislation protects the rights of individuals whose data is being held.
- Organisations that do not comply with the terms of the Data Protection Act can be prosecuted.

The eight principles of the Data Protection Act	
Personal data should:	be processed fairly and lawfully with the consent of the **data subject**
	be used only for the purpose specified
	be adequate and relevant for its intended purpose
	be accurate and up to date
	not be kept for longer than necessary
	be processed in accordance with the rights of the data subject
	be held safely and securely
	not be transferred outside the European Union without adequate protection

Data subject An individual who is the subject of personal data

- Key people referred to within the Data Protection Act include:

Key people	Who are they?
Data subject	The individual who is the subject of the personal data
Information commissioner	Responsible for enforcing the Act, promoting good practice by those responsible for processing personal data and making the general public aware of their rights under the Act
Data controller	The person within an organisation who is responsible for controlling the way in which personal data is processed

Information commissioner The title given to a government regulator who is responsible for the protection of personal data; they are responsible for enforcing the Data Protection Act

Data controller The individual in an organisation who is responsible for determining the purposes for and the manner in which personal data is processed

Copyright Designs and Patents Act 1988

- This law protects the property rights of individuals and organisations that create and produce material based on original ideas.
- Materials include computer software and are referred to as 'intellectual property'.
- The Act states that it is illegal to copy (or download) and distribute software without permission.
- When an organisation purchases a software package to install on their network, they must also purchase a **software licence** to cover the number of users (or computers) using the software.
- An organisation distributing software without a proper licence is breaking the law under this Act.
- Software producers can subscribe to organisations such as FACT (Federation against Copyright Theft) to protect against illegal use of their software.
- This legislation requires organisations to have policies ensuring employees are aware of the terms of the Act and the consequences of being in breach of it.
- Organisations are responsible for monitoring which employees have access to licensed software.

Software licence A document that provides legally binding guidance for the use and distribution of software within an organisation

Computer Misuse Act 1990

- This act is designed to protect users against computer misuse, including unauthorised access to computer systems.
- People involved in digital crimes are known as hackers.
- The Act states that it is illegal to hack computers to plant viruses or install malicious software such as **spyware**.
- It further states that it is illegal to gain unauthorised access to change passwords and computer settings (to prevent users from accessing their accounts), or modify software and data stored on a computer system.

Spyware Software that is hidden on a computer system and collects the user's information using their internet connection without their knowledge

Ethical impact of technology on society

- There are many examples to show that internet misuse is increasing on a global scale:

Misuse	Description
Usernames and passwords hacked and stolen	Used illegally to make online transactions, e.g. purchasing goods and stealing money from bank accounts
Software piracy	Users illegally download copyrighted materials from the internet
Phishing	Hackers use official-looking online adverts or emails to trick users into providing personal details
Using websites to promote violence and negative behaviour in society	Using images and videos to encourage young people to participate in anti-social behaviour
Plagiarism	Pupils copy and paste materials for coursework assignments and sign it off as their own work
Misuse of the internet in the workplace	Employees spend too much time using the internet for personal use, e.g. booking holidays, resulting in the creation of 'acceptable use of the internet' policies that employees must agree to in their employment terms and conditions
Sharing of personal data between companies without prior permission	Personal data is then open to misuse

- Our personal data can often be collected and analysed without us being fully aware of it. Examples include:

Loyalty cards used by supermarkets allow organisations to collect data about our shopping habits. This data can be used to inform their marketing and advertising departments.	CCTV cameras monitor our activity in cities and shopping centres.
Mobile phones can transmit our geographical location at any point and time so users' movements can be monitored when making or receiving phone calls.	By analysing credit or debit card transactions, customer information on shopping patterns can be sold on to third parties to target direct advertising or promote special offers.

Social networking

- Social networking involves subscribing to websites such as Facebook, Instagram, Twitter, and so on to connect with others to share photos, videos and personal messages. Some individuals misuse these platforms.
- People may search for profile pages to gain access to personal information such as addresses or phone numbers.
- Some users communicate racial and religious hatred (even though social networking sites discourage this use in their terms and conditions).
- Criminals can create an account with the intention of stealing someone's identity to commit a crime.

GPS (global positioning system)

- A GPS provides real-time information such as the geographical locations of an individual or an object.

GPS systems can raise moral and ethical issues such as:
When a user makes a mobile call or is driving a car with a GPS system, data about their location can be tracked. If this is done without consent it is an infringement on an individual's right to privacy.
When tracking individuals who need to be monitored through an electronic tracking device, e.g. offenders who are on 'home arrest' or vulnerable patients such as dementia sufferers, this can be a positive use of GPS.
Tracking of buses, taxis and company vans by organisations can be positive for customers as they are aware of arrival and departure times, but also track employee activity.

- The use of cloud-based services can also raise moral and ethical issues. Increased use of cloud servers on a global scale has implications for the security and privacy of personal data.
- Privacy laws vary in different countries, e.g. EU (European Union) laws differ from those in non-EU countries. If personal data is processed in a country with less strict laws, this could adversely impact the security of such data.

Common mistake

In questions that ask you to *evaluate*, many candidates only give one side of the story. You need to put in place an argument that clearly shows the benefits and limitations of the topic you are evaluating.

Now test yourself

TESTED ☐

1 State four principles of the Data Protection Act. [4 marks]
2 Name and describe two other laws associated with ICT. [6 marks]
3 Briefly explain the roles of information commissioners and data controllers. [4 marks]
4 Describe two ways in which social networking can be misused. [4 marks]

Revision activity

- Understand the principles of each law.
- Be able to describe the role of key people in the Data Protection Act.
- Give examples to illustrate ethical issues.

10 Impact of digital technology on employment and health and safety

Impact of digital technology on employment

Increased job opportunities

- Digital technology is continually changing the world of work and is a major influence on job opportunities.
- There are now more specialist job opportunities in hardware and software technologies, for example managing network file servers, operating systems and applications software used by organisations.
- Software engineers are required to develop and maintain programming code.
- Employment opportunities in digital media and design include app and web designers; computer game designers and developers; and computer-generated imagery (CGI) producers for the film industry.
- Forensic computer analysts work in the area of cyber crime, protecting organisations from hackers, online scams and fraud, and other malicious attacks.
- Database administrators work in large organisations, including banks and hospitals.

Job displacement

- Governments have prioritised the continued development of technology skills in the workforce.
- Further embedding digital technologies into the workplace has changed the way some jobs are carried out.
- In manufacturing, for example, the introduction of robots means that the work of a number of manual workers is now done by computer-controlled machines.
- Jobs that are highly repetitive and tedious for humans can be carried out by robots, for example car manufacturers use robots for assembling and painting cars.
- Office clerical jobs now require more skilled workers with a greater emphasis on using **generic software**, such as databases and spreadsheets, to manage their information systems.

> **Generic software** General purpose software, such as word-processing software, that is not designed specifically for a particular application

Changes in work patterns

- The development of 'smart' technology, such as smart phones, and the development of 'smart techniques' such as cloud computing have been major influences on changing work patterns.
- **Teleworking** is using ICT to work from home. This has been made possible with developments in communications technology.

> **Teleworking** Using information technology (IT) and telecommunications to work from home, replacing work-related travel

Advantages of teleworking	Disadvantages of teleworking
• Saves on travel cost and travel time to and from work for the employee. • There is no necessity for the employee to live within travelling distance of work. • The employee has flexible working hours. • The employer can employ a more global workforce with cheaper labour. • Organisations do not need to rent expensive city-centre offices and pay heating and lighting costs. • There are fewer cars on the road, which helps with pollution reduction and traffic congestion.	• Employees may feel isolated because of the loss of social interaction and teamwork. • Employees need an office at home, which may add expense. • Employees need to be disciplined to distinguish between home and work life. • Employers find it more difficult to monitor employee activity.

Exam tips

- Teleworking is not working from home, but using ICT to work from home. There is a difference!
- Refer only to jobs that involve digital technology when discussing changing work patterns.

Need for upskilling

- In a fast-changing technological work environment, people require continuous training to enable them to carry out their jobs.
- Employers need to offer relevant training courses to help improve retention levels in the workplace.

Digital-technology-related health and safety issues

REVISED

- The Health and Safety at Work etc. Act obliges employers to provide a safe working environment for employees who carry out their work using a computer.
- The law states that organisations should have a company policy on health and safety and that employees should be aware of the contents of this policy.
- The health problems associated with the regular use of computers include:

Health problem	Description	How can it be reduced?
Repetitive strain injury (RSI)	• A range of conditions affecting the muscles and joints in the neck, shoulders, arms and hands. • Caused when an employee is using the same muscle groups to perform the same actions over and over again, such as working at a keyboard all day.	• Take regular breaks • Use ergonomically designed keyboards and mice • Use appropriate furniture, e.g. adjustable swivel chairs • Use a wrist rest with the keyboard

Health problem	Description	How can it be reduced?
Eyestrain	• A common problem caused by over-exposure to computer screens. • Can lead to headaches, blurred vision and an overall deterioration to a user's eyesight.	• Use anti-glare screens • Use swivel bases on screens • Use screens that have adjustable brightness and contrast • Regular free eye tests, provided by the employer
Back pain	• Can be related to poor posture while sitting at a computer for prolonged periods. • Can lead to mobility problems.	• Use chairs that allow height adjustment and backrest tilting • Take regular breaks and regularly exercise muscles • Improve desk posture through training

Exam tip

When learning a health issue, also learn a way of minimising it.

- There are other safety issues that should be given priority in the workplace.
- Portable appliance testing (PAT testing) should be regularly carried out on hardware devices.
- Cables to and from computers should be safely organised using cable management.
- Controlled air conditioning in an office provides a more comfortable working environment for employees.
- Appropriate fire extinguishers (such as CO_2 that are suitable for electric fires) should be located in designated places in the workplace.
- No eating or drinking near computers.

Now test yourself

TESTED

1 Identify four jobs that have been created due to developments in digital technology. [4 marks]
2 What is meant by 'teleworking'? [2 marks]
3 Describe three advantages of teleworking to an employee. [6 marks]
4 State three health problems associated with ICT and explain how each can be minimised. [6 marks]
5 Identify three ways in which an organisation can assist in making the workplace safer. [3 marks]

Revision activity

- Using examples, learn how job opportunities have changed.
- Learn three advantages and three disadvantages of teleworking.
- Be able to describe a number of health issues and suggest a method to minimise each.

11 Digital applications

Gaming applications

REVISED

- Gaming applications are electronic games played on devices including games consoles, mobile phones and computers.
- Gaming has developed from the installation of discs on games consoles and playing alone to the use of the cloud and online multiplayer games.
- Educational gaming applications allow users to apply their knowledge and support their learning within a virtual world.
- Users can take on various virtual roles within a game to experience different situations, enhancing learning.
- The range of **multimedia** assets available in games can increase the motivation and communication skills of the learner.
- Games are designed with rules and increasing levels of difficulty; the user must comply with the rules and cannot move to the next level before completing the previous level.
- Used in training situations in the workplace, games can provide immediate feedback, helping users to evaluate what they have achieved.

> **Multimedia** The integration of text, graphics, video, animation and sound

> **Common mistake**
>
> Using your first-hand experience of applications such as gaming to answer questions can lead to weak answers with little or no technical terms.

Simulation applications

REVISED

- A **simulation** uses a computer model to represent a real-life object.
- Models are created from large volumes of data, along with mathematical equations, to produce 3D graphics to represent objects.
- Car manufacturers use simulations to test cars during the design stage.
- Architects use simulations to create models of new buildings before they are built.
- **Virtual reality** uses simulations to recreate 'real' experiences in a virtual world and can immerse the user in a 3D world using specialist sensory hardware devices, such as head-mounted devices.
- Simulation is used to train people for jobs with a high risk of endangering life, such as an airplane pilot.
- In the medical world, body scanners are used to produce a 3D model of a virtual patient. Surgeons can plan and practise (simulate) a particular operation on the virtual patient before carrying it out for real.

> **Simulation** A simulation uses a computer model designed to represent a 'real-life' object. Models are created from large volumes of data along with mathematical equations to produce three-dimensional graphics to represent the object
>
> **Virtual reality** VR uses simulations to recreate 'real' experiences (virtual world) using a combination of human senses, such as vision, hearing and touch, to allow the user to feel that they are experiencing the actual situation

Mobile phone applications

REVISED

- Smartphones now come with a number of preloaded applications and the ability to download further apps from app stores.
- Popular app categories include games, music, movies and instant messaging.
- Mobile apps provide opportunities for teaching and learning.

- Instant messaging allows groups of employees to create a user forum or an electronic bulletin board to communicate, share news and work together on projects.
- Schools use instant messaging to communicate with parents about forthcoming events.
- App support and regular app updates are provided by app developers for mobile devices.

Online banking

REVISED

- Customers can use the internet to access their bank account via the bank's secure website.
- They use a username and password to log on to the website.
- For additional security, customers are also asked a security question(s).
- Once online, they can carry out a range of activities, from viewing transactions and bank statements to setting up regular payments using direct debits/standing orders.

Advantages for the customer	Advantages for the bank
• Transactions can be done at home, work or on the move using mobile technology like an iPhone. • The website is available 24/7. • They access their bank account when abroad as it is available globally. • Using faster payments services allows money to be moved from one account to another immediately.	• Money is saved as fewer branches and staff are required because customers do not need to visit the bank as often. • Banks can produce e-statements, which save on paper and postage costs. • They can attract a larger customer base, as customers do not need to live close to the bank.
Drawback for the customer	**Drawback for the bank**
• The main drawback is concerns about fraud.	• The main disadvantage of this technology is the need to implement and maintain complex security systems for customer data.

Online training

REVISED

- Advances in internet and broadband communications in the workplace has allowed employers to offer online training (or web-based) programs to their employees.

Advantages of online training	Disadvantages of online training
• Employees can learn at a time that is convenient and work at their own pace. • There is no need to spend time and money travelling to training venues. • Employers can monitor employee progress through automatic tracking systems that record progress. • Multimedia assets such as animations help make the training content attractive to employees. • Virtual reality simulations offer a highly interactive and realistic form of training.	• There are limited opportunities for employees to ask questions face to face; support is often via an FAQ section. • Employees can feel isolated by the lack of human contact. • Online training does not suit all learning styles. • Each employee may be working at a different pace or even on a different module(s), which can create problems in setting deadlines for completion. • A poor internet connection or an older version of a web browser could interrupt learning.

E-commerce

- **E-commerce** is the buying and selling of products and services over the internet.

Advantages	Disadvantages
• Ordering goods online takes less time than travelling to shopping centres. • It is attractive to families who have young children or who live outside town centres as it can be difficult to make regular trips to shopping centres. • Using the internet and search engines, customers can access product reviews and price comparisons. • Customers have a wider choice and access to a greater availability of products compared to visiting their local shop(s), which may not stock a full range of products. • Businesses do not need to rent or buy expensive retail outlets as they can use out of town warehouses. • Business websites can be accessed on a global scale, thus increasing the chance of a larger customer base.	• Customers may not use an e-commerce website due to concerns over credit-card fraud. • Shopping online can rely on product images and descriptions, resulting in goods arriving that don't meet customer expectations. • There is a time delay in the delivery of goods and possibly a delivery charge. • Goods not arriving on time (or arriving faulty), particularly around Christmas, can give customers a negative experience of using e-commerce.

E-commerce A means of conducting business transactions over electronic networks, e.g. online shopping

Exam tip

- When learning about the impact of a digital application, be able to refer to the customer (or employee) and the organisation (or employer).
- Be able to refer to a range of examples when evaluating an application.

Now test yourself

TESTED

1 State three advantages of using simulation for training airline pilots. [6 marks]
2 Describe two advantages for the bank in providing online banking facilities. [4 marks]
3 Describe two concerns a customer might have in using online banking. [4 marks]
4 Briefly describe how virtual reality can assist in developing online training programs. [5 marks]
5 Describe three benefits for customers in using e-commerce. [6 marks]

Revision activity

- Learn the main features of digital applications.
- Be able to evaluate the impact of an application by referring to benefits and drawbacks.

12 Designing solutions

End user involvement in prototyping

REVISED

- Prototyping involves ongoing input from the end user.
- It refers to the creation of incomplete versions of a product, which can be used to support the development of the final product.
- There are two main approaches to prototyping:

Evolutionary	Throwaway
The incomplete version of the product is continually refined and developed until a complete solution is available.	Used to support discussions between the end user and the developer, e.g. to help determine end user requirements. It does not form part of the final solution.

Prototype A model of a system being developed; it may not be fully functional

Evolutionary prototype A prototype that is reviewed and improved and eventually forms the final system solution

Throwaway prototype A prototype that does not become part of the final system solution

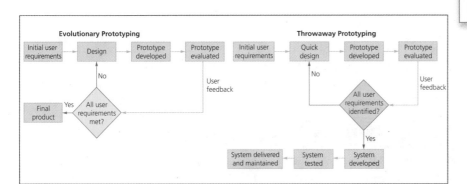

Evolutionary prototyping versus throwaway prototyping

Advantages of prototyping	Disadvantages of prototyping
• Increased end user involvement so the product is more likely to meet the end user needs • Changes/problems are detected early, reducing the cost of correction	• End user involvement may lead to constantly changing requirements • Not suited to all types of applications

- The end user is the person (people) who will use the system when it is completed.
- A **user requirement document** details the end user's needs, i.e. the tasks they expect to complete using the system.
- End users provide feedback after every refinement of the **prototype**. Changes are made to the prototype after feedback from the end user.

User requirement document A document that details what the end user expects the system to do; it often forms part of a contract between the developer and the end user

Common mistake

Remember that end users are involved in all stages of prototype development. In other development approaches, the end user may only be involved at the beginning of the process, to identify user requirements.

Exam tip

Remember that not all approaches to prototyping lead to the evolution of the completed application.

Multimedia design elements

- The **target audience** must be identified as this will help determine how the **user interface** will be designed.
- A user requirements document provides a list of systems requirements needed to ensure the system operates effectively. The requirements must be measurable and written in a language that is easy for the end user to understand.
- **Navigation structure diagrams** show various pathways end users can take through a multimedia package. They make use of arrows or lines to show links between internal and external pages.

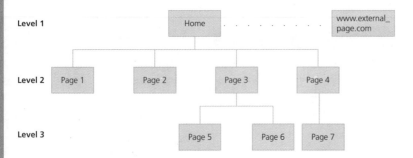

A navigation structure diagram

- **Storyboards** are used to show the content of all pages/screens in the applications. They include details of any **image sources**, text and other multimedia elements and should be detailed enough to support **third-party implementation**.

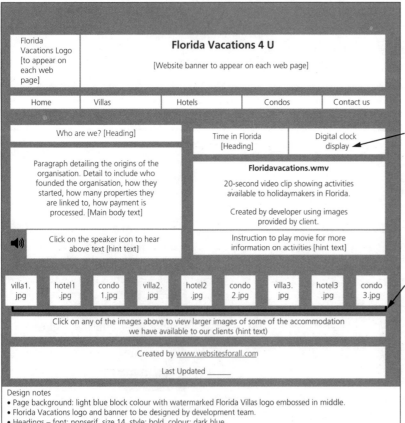

A detailed storyboard

Target audience The demographic group for whom an application is being developed

User interface Any part of the system that the user can interact with; this includes data capture forms, menus and buttons

Navigation structure diagram A diagram that illustrates the various pathways a user can take through a multimedia application

Storyboard A diagrammatic illustration showing the content and layout of individual pages in a multimedia application

Image sources Details of any graphic elements to be incorporated into an application, in the form of file names, web location or a description of the image if it is to be created by the developer

Third-party implementation The creation of a product by someone other than the original designer

Scripted elements Extracts of code, often included as part of an HTML document, that, when activated, can allow the end user to interact with the application and amend the contents being displayed

Interactive elements Elements in a package that prompt interaction from the end user

- **Movie/animation timelines** are used to illustrate the content and length of individual scenes in the movie/animation. They also include details of any special effects or transitions applied between scenes and any sound playing throughout.

> **Movie timeline** A diagrammatic representation that shows the content of a movie, frame by frame

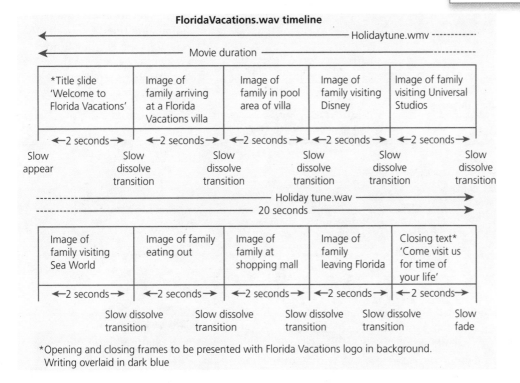

A movie timeline

- A good storyboard contains details of any **scripted** or **interactive elements**. This can be in the form of an algorithm or other description of how elements are expected to behave.

Database design elements

REVISED

A **data dictionary** is a file that details the structure of data held in a database.

- It includes details such as table names, **attributes**, validation methods and other controls used to support correct data entry, characteristics of each attribute (for example, whether it is a key field or a required field), field length and data type.

Form and report **wireframe diagrams** detail the input, output and often the navigation screens to be used in a database application.

- They include details on the screen layout, for example: input fields to be included on each form or report; calculated fields and their associated formulas; and the location and format of any specialised control elements, such as drop-down menus.
- They show the position of each element on the form or report in addition to the font, style and colour of any text elements.
- They also show the location of any specialised interface elements, such as navigation buttons or graphical elements.

> **Data dictionary** A file containing details relating to the structure of data held in a database
>
> **Attribute** The heading given to each item of data stored about a single database entity
>
> **Wireframe diagram** A tool used to show the layout of input and output screens in a digital application

Entity-relationship diagrams show how the various entities represented within the database will be linked together by relationships. The most common types of relationships between database tables are:

Relationship type	Description	Diagram
one-to-one _____	e.g. adult 1 is married to adult 2	adult 1 — adult 2
one-to-many —<	e.g. one parent can have many children	parent —< children
many-to-many >—<	e.g. a grandparent can have more than one grandchild and each grandchild can have more than one grandparent	grand parent >—< grand child

Entity-relationship diagram
A diagram used to illustrate how various entities (items represented in a database) are linked together

Exam tips

Questions on entity-relationship diagrams may ask you to identify the types of relationships required between tables in a database. To help determine the direction of a one-to-many relationship, identify where the key field from one table is used to create a link with another (this is where the many relationship will exist).

Now test yourself

TESTED ☐

1 Describe how end user involvement in prototyping can be an advantage and a disadvantage to the developer. [4 marks]
2 List the characteristics of a good user requirements document. [3 marks]
3 A good design document supports third-party implementation. Explain the term 'third-party implementation'. [2 marks]

Revision activity

- Learn the definition of the term 'prototype' and the difference between a throwaway and evolutionary prototype.
- Learn the main elements included in the design documents for multimedia and database applications.
- Review examples of a multimedia storyboard, data dictionary, report and query wireframes and entity-relationship diagrams.

13 Digital development considerations

Human–computer interfaces

Graphical user interface

Description	Advantages	Disadvantages
Allows interactions through the selection of on-screen options and through the use of a WIMP environment (see below)	• Intuitive, as icons use familiar images • Users do not need technical elements of a computer to use it • Shortcuts can be created by more experienced users	• Additional processing power, storage and RAM are often required • Powerful graphics cards are required • Can be restrictive for expert users

> **Human–computer interface**
> The use of digital technology to support communication between end users and computers

> **Exam tip**
> Know the advantages and disadvantages of each interface type and be able to identify appropriate applications for each.

- **WIMP** stands for:

  Window: an area on the desktop showing actions being performed by the user

  Icon: a small picture representing a shortcut to a task or application

  Menu: a method of grouping related tasks

  Pointer: an on-screen icon that moves in response to a mouse or similar input device.

> **Graphical user interface**
> (GUI) A user interface that provides windows, menus, icons and pointers so that the user can operate it
>
> **WIMP** Windows Icon Menu Pointer
>
> **Natural language interface**
> A means of interacting with digital technology using everyday language

Natural language interfaces

Description	Advantages	Disadvantages
Support interaction through the use of everyday language (via spoken or typed instructions)	• No need to learn specialised commands • Suitable for users with limited mobility • Support hands-free interactions	• It takes time to 'train' to recognise a user's voice • Applications may not respond to all voices • The command bank can be limited • Increased RAM, ROM and processing power may be required

Motion tracking interfaces

Description	Advantages	Disadvantages
Use sensors or optical methods to convert movement into digital signals for input into a digital device/application; optical methods can use cameras, reflective markers, sensors or LEDs to help track motion	• Make interaction more realistic • Allow inexperienced users to interact with the application • Support users who have issues with fine motor control	• Still a new technology so not widely available • Can be expensive

Touchscreen

Description	Advantages	Disadvantages
Interactions can be through the use of a stylus or direct connection with the screen using your fingers as a selection tool (See Chapter 5 for the features of touchscreen technology.)	• On-screen keyboards can be included to help improve portability • Intuitive to use	• Can be easily damaged • Screens can be small, making interactions with small icons and keys difficult • Technology is still relatively expensive • Can be difficult for visually impaired users

Using sensors to support motion tracking

> **Motion tracking interface**
> Interface that converts movement into digital signals

Common mistake

Often when asked about the advantages of a touchscreen interface, students will talk about how it can be used by anyone regardless of the language they speak. This is because the interface tends to be graphical, but remember that this is a software-related advantage and is not related to the hardware.

Developing accessible digital applications

REVISED

- Accessibility refers to the ability to personalise digital applications to support their use.
- Many digital applications come with specialised settings that can enhance accessibility, for example, on-screen magnifiers, text narrators or the ability to alter the sensitivity of a touch pad.
- **W3C (World Wide Web Consortium)** have established a set of standards aimed at improving the accessibility of internet digital applications such as mobile phone apps.

> **W3C (World Wide Web Consortium)** A standards organisation whose focus is on ensuring accessibility of digital applications

Exam tip

Be familiar with the role played by the W3C in the development of accessibility standards associated with internet and mobile phone applications.

Developing cross-platform digital applications

REVISED

- Applications that support operation on different hardware and software **platforms** are **cross-platform applications**.
- Developers must consider that not all members of their target audience will use the same technology. They must remember that what looks good on one may not look good on another.
- To ensure cross-platform compatibility, platform-specific versions of an application must be developed. During development, consideration should be given to any parts that can be reused.
- The app must be fully tested on all target platforms.

> **Platform** The hardware or software (or both) that supports the operation of an application
>
> **Cross-platform application** An application designed to operate successfully on more than one platform

Now test yourself answers and glossary at www.hoddereducation.co.uk/myrevisionnotes

Improving cross-platform compatibility

- **Plugin** software can add functionality to an existing application.
- Where plugins are required, the developer should provide the user with a link to the appropriate download site.
- **PDF** files are accessible on any platform so should be used where possible.
- **Optimised** file formats can be used to support the smooth loading of pages or screens on a digital application, but it is important to remember that not all file formats are supported on every platform. Plugins may be required to support the integration of some optimised file types, but expecting the end user to download a large number of plugins is not advisable.
- An optimised file is one that has been **compressed**, i.e. any unnecessary data has been removed to reduce the file size.
- The optimised file formats listed in the table are supported by most platforms. See Chapter 1 for additional information.

Video file formats	Image file formats	Sound file formats
- Flash video (.flv) - AVI (.avi) - Quicktime (.mov) - MP4 (.mp4)	- Jpeg (.jpg) - GIF (.gif) - TIFF (.tif) - PNG (.png)	- MP3 (.mp3) - WAV (.wav) is supported by most browsers, although is not a compressed file format

Plugin Software that adds features to an application once installed

PDF (Portable Document Format) A piece of software that supports presentation of text, graphics and hyperlinks on a range of platforms

Optimisation When files are compressed to facilitate storage or electronic transmission

Optimised Code that uses the minimum of resources during operation and that is efficient in terms of speed of operation

Compression The reduction of file size through the removal of unnecessary data

Now test yourself

1 Describe the main features of a GUI (graphical user interface). [4 marks]
2 Describe the advantages of using motion tracking interfaces in relation to a gaming application. [2 marks]
3 Describe how touchscreen interfaces can be used to improve the accessiblity of an application. [2 marks]
4 Describe the term 'cross-platform' in relation to the development of digital applications. [2 marks]
5 List two ways a developer can help to improve the cross-platform compatibility of their application. [2 marks]

Revision activity

- Produce a mind map detailing the features of each of the interface types identified in this chapter.
- Make a list of possible applications for each of these interfaces.
- Produce revision cards relating to the importance of developing cross-platform applications and methods used by developers to improve cross-platform compatibility of applications.
- Copy out and learn the table of optimised file formats and the file types they support.

13 Digital development considerations

14 Multimedia applications

Multimedia and interactive features

REVISED

- Most digital applications incorporate a range of multimedia and interactive features designed to enhance the end user's experience when using the application.
- Interaction is determined by the way the user implements hardware and software to view output and generate input to an application, often in response to output presented to them.

Multimedia features	Interactive features
<ul><li>The use of text and images to enhance the application content</li><li>Stored video and/or sound files</li><li>Live sound and/or video streaming (see Chapter 1)</li><li>Interactive sound and/or video, e.g. through video conferencing or VoIP</li></ul>	<ul><li>Virtual tours or 3D interactive displays</li><li>Live interactive video chats</li><li>Hyperlinks to other pages or websites</li><li>Twitter feeds and memes</li><li>Playing multimedia elements</li><li>Thumbnail and/or roll over images</li><li>Form fillings and option selection</li></ul>

Common mistakes

Many students provide definitions of the terms 'multimedia' and 'interactivity', but are not able to give appropriate examples of how each is used in a given application. Be able to give examples of how both features enhance user experiences with digital applications in each of the areas covered in this chapter.

Multimedia and interactivity in e-commerce

REVISED

- Examples of some of the interactive and multimedia features used by e-commerce sites include:
  - product reviews posted by customers
  - watch lists/product tracking
  - seller or product ratings
  - secure online payment methods
  - live bidding and alert systems
  - **push technology** to send customer alerts
  - sharing product information on other media applications
  - help systems and dispute resolution systems
  - image display tools
  - shopping carts.

> **Push technology** Allows information to be delivered automatically to recipient, e.g. pop-ups

Advantages	Disadvantages
<ul><li>Customers are able to see others' views of the product/seller</li><li>Stock levels can be checked before ordering and orders can be tracked online</li><li>Key words can be used to search quickly for desired items</li><li>Image display tools allow users to clearly see the item they are purchasing</li><li>Bank details are not available to other parties, and third-party organisations who provide secure payment methods help users with payment disputes</li><li>Items can be monitored in bidding interactions</li><li>Alerts can be sent to customers via pop-ups or emails</li><li>Product information can be shared with others via email links and social media posts</li><li>Shopping carts allow users to save items and complete their purchases later</li></ul>	<ul><li>Review postings are often limited in word length, and tend to be subjective – not all users apply the same standards to the products they are buying</li><li>Not all sellers provide tracking data</li><li>Key word searches are reliant on the seller using the same key words to describe the item</li><li>Not all users have access to electronic payment methods</li><li>Constant alerts can be annoying</li><li>Images may not always show clearly on all devices</li><li>If items are reserved indefinitely in shopping carts they may be unavailable to other customers</li></ul>

- More information on e-commerce can be found in Chapter 10.

Multimedia and interactivity in social media

REVISED

- 'Social media' refers to the use of digital technology to support the creation and sharing of multimedia content on an online platform.
- Increase used of social media has led to the creation of **virtual communities** where content is submitted from members all over the world.
- Social media applications are generally Web 2.0-based and delivered via web-based or mobile telephone applications.
- Members share content with each other, post their own ideas and sometimes even post products for sale.
- Some of the interactive and multimedia features available in social media applications are:
  - user-generated content – updated any time and location check-ins
  - live streaming and **chat clients**
  - **call-to-action buttons**
  - personalised pages and content sharing
  - free **web space**
  - user profiles.

Virtual communities
A group of individuals who communicate in an online forum

Chat clients An application that supports interactive real-time chat between two participants

Call-to-action button
A clickable link on a social media page that prompts the user to take some form of action

Web space An area of a host's server made available to an end user for the storage of their content

- Advantages and disadvantages of the various interactive and multimedia features available on social media sites include:

Advantages	Disadvantages
<ul><li>User-generated content creates a feeling of connectivity</li><li>Live streaming is a new and exciting way to share ideas</li><li>End users can control who has access to their profile data and posts and who they accept as link members in their virtual community</li><li>Users have access to the wider global community</li><li>Location searches can be used to improve personal connectivity</li><li>Web space is free</li><li>Chats, messages and other posts can be read at the user's leisure, but interactivity is also supported; chat content can appear for a timed period only</li><li>A wider audience is available for the promotion of events/products</li><li>Graphical representations can be used to provide immediate and easily understood responses to online content</li></ul>	<ul><li>Can be a forum for abuse and has the potential to be intrusive and distracting if not properly managed</li><li>Extensive access via mobile digital devices may be expensive as they tend to be media rich and require excessive data downloads</li><li>Caution should be exercised when revealing personal details</li><li>Social media sites retain the rights to posted content</li><li>Can lead to isolation</li><li>Not all members of the target audience may have access to social media</li><li>Location posting can compromise the safety of the user</li><li>Some applications require addition plugins</li></ul>

Multimedia and interactivity in gaming

REVISED

- Gamers can interact with gaming applications using a wide range of peripheral devices; or indeed some now allow interactions without any peripherals.
- Interactivity begins now before users even begin game play as many games allow users to alter **game settings** and characters.
- Examples of interactivity and multimedia in gaming applications include:
  - various forms of audio and visual **feedback** and input, for example on-screen character movement in response to user input, or audio input and output used to support input of user instructions or feedback following an on-screen event
  - 3D interaction with gaming applications through the use of sensors and virtual reality interactions
  - customising settings and characters to help personalise gaming experience, for example in **role-play game** applications
  - adjusting the display view to support game play from various angles in the scenario.

Game settings An area of a gaming application where the user can adjust game elements, e.g. sound levels, controls and even create their own characters

Feedback Situation where input is affected by output from a digital application

Role-play game A gaming environment where the end user plays the game in the persona of a character from the game; all interactions with the game are in that persona

Advantages of interactivity in gaming	Disadvantages of interactivity in gaming
<ul><li>Increased interactivity can enhance the gaming experience</li><li>Provision of immediate feedback encourages alertness and improves attention to game play</li><li>Ability to adjust setting and characters helps personalise the game</li><li>High-quality multimedia enhances the gaming experience</li><li>Use of specialised peripherals can make the game more realistic</li></ul>	<ul><li>Incorporating high-quality multimedia elements increases storage demands</li><li>In online gaming applications the user is dependent upon a reliable telecommunications link</li><li>Code is complex and programs tend to be long, leading to increased costs</li><li>Demands on processing elements and hardware devices increase</li><li>Specialised input devices are often needed for realistic interactions</li></ul>

Now test yourself answers and glossary at www.hoddereducation.co.uk/myrevisionnotes

Multimedia and interactivity in generic applications

REVISED

- Multimedia and interactive content is now expected in our interactions with most digital applications, for example digital TV, mobile phone apps, gaming consoles, controls for home utilities, and so on. All of these applications and interfaces provide us with graphical user interfaces, sound feedback and, in many cases, specialised input devices.

Advantages of multimedia and interactivity in generic applications	Disadvantages of multimedia and interactivity in generic applications
• Interactive media engages the user and helps with information retention • Communication between users on some devices and applications can be supported, e.g. many online booking applications now offer users the opportunity to communicate with a support agent via a messaging tool • Push technology allows application managers to present their message to users at any time and from any location • Content on multimedia applications can be updated easily and made available to all users quickly • Interfaces tend to be intuitive and therefore appeal to a wider audience	• Specialised hardware and software is often needed to access interactive multimedia applications • Users/members of the target audience may not access all of the information being presented to them • Some users may find the messages presented by push technology to be intrusive • Some applications require a high level of maintenance on the part of the development team • Technical experience may be necessary to support the creation and maintenance of the interactive multimedia application • Users may find the cost of the specialised hardware required to be prohibitive • Complex code is required to support the development of the application • Multimedia applications demand increased processing power, memory and storage

Now test yourself

TESTED

1. List three examples of interactive features and three examples of multimedia features application developers can include in a digital application. [6 marks]
2. List three advantages and three disadvantages of the use of interactive multimedia in social networking applications. [6 marks]
3. Chose an e-commerce application you are familiar with and list the interactive and multimedia elements it provides for users. [4 marks]
4. Identify three ways that interactivity and multimedia can help enhance the gaming experience of a user playing a computer game. [3 marks]

Revision activity

- Produce a short presentation on the use of interactive and multimedia elements in any of the following applications: e-commerce, social media, gaming or generic applications. If you have time, work with friends and split the topics, then present your findings to each other.
- Chose any digital application you are familiar with and produce a list of the interactive and multimedia features it provides for end users.
- Learn the definitions of the key words associated with this topic. Write the terms out on a blank page and then test yourself by writing the definition beside the appropriate key term.

Exam tip

Use the appropriate key words when answering questions, especially QWC questions. This will help ensure your answers will be assessed as being in the higher mark band.

15 Multimedia authoring

Multimedia authoring

REVISED

- Multimedia authoring refers to the development of any application that uses a range of media types to present information.
- Media types incorporated into the application may include sound, video, animation, graphics, text.
- It makes use of **hypertext** and **hypermedia** and scripted elements to support non-linear user progression through the application.
  - ○ 'Hypertext' refers to the use of text to provide links to related content.
  - ○ 'Hypermedia' refers to the use of multimedia elements to provide links to related content.
- Multimedia packages can be developed using specialised authoring applications or using code such as **HTML**.

> **Hypertext** Text that can provide links to related content in a multimedia application
>
> **Hypermedia** The use of media including text, graphics, video and sound elements of an application to provide links to related content in a multimedia application

Multimedia authoring software

REVISED

- Multimedia authoring applications contain predefined elements to support the development of packages.
- Multimedia authoring software can provide users with a WYSIWYG (what you see is what you get) environment to support visual development of the application using drag and drop tools.
- It does not require the end user to have any underlying knowledge of a programming language when developing an application.
- It automatically generates the underlying code for the application as new content is added to the page.
- Some of the features provided by multimedia authoring applications include:
  - ○ template provision – to help ensure consistency of presentation across all pages in the application
  - ○ content management – to support organisation and location of content during the development stages; some content management tools automatically update hyperlinks if the developer moves content between folders (within the application)
  - ○ form tools; hyperlinks and hotspots; and wizards.

> **HTML** (hypertext markup language) The language used to define the structure of webpages; it is often combined with CSS and JavaScript to create hypermedia applications presented to users via browser software for the World Wide Web

Advantages of using a web authoring application	Disadvantages of using a web authoring application
• Very little technical or programming knowledge is required • Has an intuitive interface • Links can automatically update when content is moved around	• Limited functionality – some coding may be needed if complex interactions are required • Templates can restrict development and lead to unoriginal developments

Using HTML to create a website

- Taking a coded approach to the development of applications allows the developer greater opportunity to 'tweak' page layout.
- HTML (hypertext markup language) is a text-based language used to describe layout of content displayed using web browser applications.
- It uses **tags** to describe page content.
- The basic structure of an HTML document is shown in the following diagram.

> **Tags** Abbreviations used in HTML to describe the main elements of a web page
>
> **Metadata** Data which describes other data. In an HTML document, metadata is defined inside the <head> </head> tags

Here you are identifying the version of HTML being used – in this case HTML5.

<HTML> tag opens the document – you will see a matching </tag> at the end of the page to indicate the document is being closed.

The <head> tag can contain information about the document. It currently holds the document title but it can hold other elements of **metadata** such as any scripts or styles or the character set used in the document. We are only concerned with the title tag at this stage.

The <title> tag allows us to provide the user with additional information about the page they are viewing.

The body section is used to define any multimedia elements which will appear in the browser window.

```
Basic structure of an HTML document
<!doctype HTML>
<HTML>
  <head>
    <title>
    </title>
  </head>
<body>
<!--Add HTML here for webpage content-->
</body>
</HTML>
```

> **Fallback text** An error message in the event that a file cannot be played by the browser

HTML tags and functions

- HTML tags to change browser and text display:

Tag	Example	How it affects display
<title> </title>	<title> First HTML Page</title>	Will display the words 'First HTML Page' in the tab for the browser window displaying the web page
<h1> </h1>	<h1> Welcome to my web page </h1>	Will display the words 'Welcome to my web page' using a predefined heading style (h1); there are six heading tags (h1–h6) – h1 is the largest text size
<div> </div>	<div align="center"> <h1> Welcome to my web page </h1> </div>	Used to define sections (divisions) in HTML pages so styles can be applied to specific sections of a page only – in this case the text will be centre aligned
<p> </p>	<p> This is the first paragraph of text on my web page. It is an introduction. </p>	Defines a section of text as a paragraph – most browsers will add a space before and after a <p> element to separate it from the rest of the text
<b> </b> <i> </i> <u> </u>	<p> <b> <i> <u>This is the first paragraph of text on my web page. It is an introduction. </b> </i> </u></p>	In this instance, the text within the paragraph will display in bold, italic and underline format
</br>	<p> This is the first paragraph of </br> text on my web page. It is an introduction. </p>	Using this tag forces the browser to insert a line break in the middle of a paragraph – the </br> tag does not need a paired opening tag in the way the other tags do

● HTML tags for displaying graphics and video and inserting sound files:

Tag	Example	How it affects display
<img>	<img src="buildings.png" alt="city skyline" height="200" width="200"> src identifies where the image is located alt will display alternate text for the image if the viewer places the cursor over the image <img> can also be used to integrate animations into the body of an HTML document	Displays an image called building.gif. Image width is 200 pixels and image height is 200 pixels. If the user of the multimedia application places a cursor over the image, the text 'city skyline' will appear.
<audio> </audio>	<audio src="music.mp3" autoplay> </audio> <audio controls> <source src="music.mp3" type="audio/mpeg"> This file type is not supported by your browser. </audio>	Supports automatic playback of the sound file music.mp3. The audio tag allows you to insert **fallback text**. Inserts audio controls with the sound file so the user can select to play the music file or not.
<video> </video>	<video width="200" height="200" controls> <source src="mymovie.mp4" type="video/mp4"> This file type is not supported by your browser. </video> <img dynsrc="mymovie.avi" start="fileopen">	Embeds an external video called mymovie.mp4 into an HTML5 document. MP4 file formats are supported by Google Chrome. Inserts videos for automatic playback to be viewed in Internet Explorer. If you prefer your user to have control over the playback of movie files you can add a hyperlink to the original movie file.

● HTML tags for displaying tables and lists:

Tag	Example	How it affects display
<table> </table> <tr> </tr> <th> </th> <td> </td>	<table bgcolor="blue" border="1" bordercolor="black"> <tr> <th>Student</th> <th>Score</th> </tr> <tr> <td>Jack</td> <td>90</td> </tr> <tr> <td>Jane</td> <td>91</td> </tr> </table>	Creates the following table of information. | Student	Score | |---|---|
Jack	90
Jane	91	

Now test yourself answers and glossary at www.hoddereducation.co.uk/myrevisionnotes

Tag	Example	How it affects display

`<ol> </ol>`	`<ol type="1">`
	
	`<li>Alexander</li>`
	`<li>Max</li>`
	`<li>Emma</li>`
	`</ol>`
		Displays an ordered list. In this case the ol tag has the '1' type (or style) assigned to it so items in the list will be numbered.
		
		Here, the list displayed would be:
		1 Alexander
		2 Max
		3 Emma
		
		Other styles include 'a', 'A', 'i', 'I' representing list styles labelled in lower case, upper case, lower case Roman numerals and upper case Roman numerals

`<ul> </ul>`	`<ul style="list-style-type:disc">`
	
	`<li>Alexander</li>`
	`<li>Max</li>`
	`<li>Emma</li>`
	`</ul>`
		Displays an unordered list. In this case the `<ul>` tag has a disc style assigned to it so the list will be displayed as a bulleted list of names using solid bullet points (disc). Other styles include circle, square or none.

- HTML tags for commenting and adding hyperlinks:

Tag	Example	How it affects display
`<!-- -->`	`<!-- Any comments to help with the understanding of HTML code can be inside this tag -->`	The developer can add comments alongside their code and they will not display in the browser.
`<a> </a>`	`<a href="http://www.mypage.com">Click here </a>`	The example displays a text-based hyperlink. The user clicks on the words 'Click here' to visit the website.

Common mistakes

It is easy to read short extracts of HTML code and understand its placement of content on a web page. It is important that you are familiar with all tags and can identify errors in their use. You should also be familiar with the structure of an HTML document.

Static web pages Pages that are presented to the user in the form that they were created; they tend to end with the extension .htm or .html

Advantages and disadvantages of using HTML to create a multimedia solution

Advantages	Disadvantages
- Most developers are familiar with HTML - It is supported by all browsers - It is free and no additional software is needed	- Updating links can be difficult if content is not managed effectively - Can only create **static pages**; if a **dynamic page** is required then additional script (e.g. Java script) is needed - Many lines of script are needed for even the most basic of pages

Content management

REVISED

- Many web-authoring applications provide the end user with a tool to support the management of application content such as pages or multimedia elements.
- They will allow links to be automatically updated when content is moved around within the application.
- Developers who are using a coding approach are required to manually update pathways to links if content is relocated within the folder structure of the application. Well-organised folders can help with this process.

Dynamic web pages Pages where the presentation can be changed by a user's interactions with the application; they tend to end with the extensions .php, .asp or .jsp

Using CSS

- **CSS** (cascading style sheets) refers to a language used to describe styles within an HTML document.
- Styles defined using CSS can refer to colour, font, text size, headings and paragraphs within a web page.

> **CSS** (cascading style sheets) A language used to describe the style of an HTML document; it describes how specified elements will be displayed

Using scripting in multimedia authoring software

REVISED

- JavaScript is often used to improve the interactivity of multimedia applications. It can be incorporated into an HTML document in a number of ways:
  - using the <script> </script> tags to incorporate it into the body of the HTML document
  - using the .js file extension to link to external files containing the script
  - placing the script in the head section of an HTML document and then activating/calling the script from within the <body> section.

Sequencing, selection and repetition

- **Sequencing**: all lines of code run one after another and all lines of code are executed. The order of execution of the script never changes.
- **Selection**: used in instances where only some lines of code need to be executed and only if a certain condition is met. If the condition is not met, the code is not executed.
- **Repetition**: causes lines of code to be executed again and again; either a specific number of times, until a condition is met or while a condition is met.
- The table below provides some examples of each coding structure using JavaScript.

> **Sequencing** Where lines of code are designed to run one after another from the beginning to the end
>
> **Selection** Where only some lines of code need to be run and only if a certain condition is met
>
> **Repetition** Where select lines of code can be executed over and over again, either a set number of times or until a condition is met

Sequencing	Selection	Repetition

`<script>`
`var x, y, z;`
`x=10;`
`y=34;`
`z=x+y;`
`window.alert("The answer is" +z);`
`</script>`
	`for (i = 0; i < 4; i++) {`
	`membersdisplay += members[i] + ", ";`
	`}`
		`<script>`
		`function myFunction( ) {`
		`var hour = new Date().getHours()`
		`if(hour < 21) {`
		`alert("You still have time to study");`
		`} else {`
		`alert("Perhaps now you should relax for the evening");`
		`}`
		`}`
		`</script>`

Event-driven programming

- Uses the user's interactions with the application (for example through mouse clicks) to determine how an application is presented to the user.
- A JavaScript example is provided below. JavaScript is included within the body tags and used to change the on-screen display following the execution of an **event** by the end user (button click):

```
<button onclick="document.getElementByid
('myimage').src='building2.jpg'">Change the
building</button>

<img id="myimage" src="building.jpg"
style="width:100px">

<button onclick="document.getElementByid
('myimage').src='building.jpg'">Restore
building</button>
```

Event-driven programming
Where events such as the user's interaction with an application element can determine how the application is presented to the end user

Now test yourself

TESTED ☐

1 Explain why content and folder management is an important part of the development of multimedia applications. [2 marks]
2 Explain the term 'metadata'. [1 mark]
3 Give two advantages and two disadvantages of using HTML to create a multimedia solution. [4 marks]
4 Explain the difference between a static and a dynamic web page. [2 marks]
5 Expand the acronym CSS. [1 mark]
6 Explain two methods web developers can use to incorporate scripted elements into an HTML document. [2 marks]
7 Explain each of the following coding constructs and how each can affect how code is executed.
   (a) Sequencing [2 marks]
   (b) Selection [2 marks]
   (c) Repetition [2 marks]
8 Explain the term 'event-driven programming' in the context of multimedia development. [2 marks]

Revision activity

- View the source code of a range of websites accessed on the internet and look for tags you are familiar with from your studies of this topic. Examine how the tags translate into on-screen displays in your browser window.
- Learn the structures, spelling and functions of HTML tags listed in this chapter.
- Practise integrating scripted elements into basic web pages to ensure you are familiar with the main coding constructs covered in this topic.
- Produce summary notes relating to the main theoretical topics covered in this chapter.

16 Database development

Relational databases

- Relational databases can help overcome some of the issues associated with storing data in a flat-file database.
- Data is stored in more than one table. Each table represents entities about whom/which data is to be stored.
- Tables representing entities can be linked.
- Linking tables helps:
  - reduce **data redundancy** (since data is not repeated unnecessarily)
  - increase **data integrity** (since data is only recorded once, it need only be updated once).
- This extract from a table shows how a flat-file database can lead to problems with data redundancy and reduced integrity:

> **Data redundancy**
> The unnecessary repetition of data in a database
>
> **Data integrity** The accuracy and consistency of data stored in a database

Member ID	Surname	First Name	House Number	Street	Town	Post Code	Game ID	Game Title	Platform
1	Smith	James	3	Main Street	Newtown	BT19 7YT		FIFA 17	Xbox One S
1	Smith	James	3	Main Street	Newtown	BT19 7YT	7	Minecraft	Xbox One S
1	Smith	James	3	Main Street	Newtown	BT19 7YT	2	Football Manager	Xbox One S
2	Jones	Amy	78	High street	Oldtown	BT18 6HY	5	NBA2K17	PS4
2	Jones	Amy	78	High street	Oldtown	BT18 6HY	9	SIMS 4	PS4
3	Brown	Jack	42	South Square	Oldtown	BT18 8PJ	6	Lego Jurassic World	PC
3	Brown	Jack	42	South Square	Oldtown	BT18 8PJ	3	Ratchet Plant	PC
4	Andrews	Sarah	6	Hill Street	Newtown	BT19 6GY	4	Marvel Pinball	Xbox One S
4	Andrews	Sharon	6	Hill Street	Newtown	BT19 6GY	8	NHl17	Xbox One S

Reduction in data integrity: errors have been introduced when entering data relating to member number 4.

Data redundancy: some data has been entered more than once (unnecessarily).

- The data shown in the extract of a flat file data database above can be represented more effectively in the following relational database format:

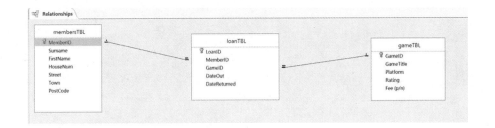

- Using this relational format:
  - Sarah Andrews' details would only need to be entered once into the database, helping preserve data integrity
  - members' details and game details would only need to be entered once into their respective tables, reducing data redundancy
  - loanTBL can be used to record details of game loans without the need to enter full member or game details each time a loan occurs (MemberID and GameID are used to identify the relevant entities associated with each loan).

Relational database features

REVISED

- When creating relational databases the following features are to be considered:

Entities

- An entity is an item that is represented in a database. The detail related to an entity is stored in a table within a database. In the example above, customer would be an example of an entity.

Fields and key fields

- A field is the name associated with a single attribute stored about an entity in a database. In the example above, GameTitle would be an example of an entity in gameTBL.

- A **key field** is a field used to uniquely identify an entity in a database, for example MemberID, LoadID or GameID in the previous example.

- A foreign key field is a key field from one table that appears in another table in order to create a link between the two tables in a relational database.

> **Key field** The field that uniquely identifies one record

Data types

- When creating database fields it is important to ensure you select the most appropriate data type for any attributes in each database table.

- Data types are covered in more detail in Chapter 3, but the most relevant data types to be aware of include: text, number, date/time, currency, autonumber, yes/no, OLE object, hyperlink, attachment, calculated, **lookup list**.

> **Lookup list** A list of data that can be used (or 'looked up') to provide all available values for a given data field

Field sizes

- When creating fields for any database application it is important to consider maximum field sizes to help ensure optimum use of the data storage allocated to the database.

Validation methods

- Data validation helps ensure that the date entered into a database field is present, the correct type, within the correct range and the correct length. The main types of validation checks include:
  - presence check: ensures the field cannot be left blank
  - length check: ensures the data entered is the correct number of characters
  - type check: ensures the data entered is of the correct type, for example, date of birth should be date/time
  - format check: ensure the data entered matches a predetermined pattern, for example dd/mm/yyyy for date of birth
  - range check: ensures the data entered is within an upper and lower limiting set of values.

Input masks

- Input masks can be used to control data entry as they help ensure the user adheres to a particular format when data is being entered.
- Some examples of input mask controls include:

0	0 to 9 only can be entered (+ or – NOT accepted). Data entry is required.
9	0 to 9 can be entered or SPACE (+ or – NOT accepted). Data entry is NOT required.
#	0 to 9 accepted, SPACE accepted, + or – accepted. Data entry NOT required.
L	A–Z accepted. Data entry required.
?	A–Z accepted. Data entry NOT required.
A	A–Z or 0–9 accepted. Data entry required.
a	A–Z or 0–9 accepted. Data entry NOT required.
&	Any character or space accepted. Data entry required.
C	Any character or space accepted. Data entry NOT required.
<	All characters following this symbol will be converted to lower case.
>	All characters following this symbol will be converted to upper case.

Lookup lists

- Lookup lists can help reduce the chance of error during data entry by providing the user with a list of options to select from during the data entry-stage.
- This helps ensure that only data from the specified set of values can be entered into the field and helps reduce the chance of transcription or transposition errors occurring as data is being manually typed into a database field.

An example of a lookup list being used to enter data

Relationships

- Relationships formed between database tables can help reduce data redundancy and increase data integrity.
- Relationship types can be one-to-one, one-to-many or many-to-many.
- **You should review your notes from Chapter 12 on relationship types and entity-relationship diagrams at this point.**
- When creating a relationship it is important that you always pay appropriate attention to the need to 'enforce referential integrity' or the need to enforce **cascade-update** or **cascade-delete** in the database structures.

> **Cascade-update/cascade-delete** Ensure that changes made in the linked table are also shown in the primary table

Forms for data input

- Forms are used to collect data from people and are often used in databases as a means to enter, view or modify data. Data entered into a form is automatically entered into the relevant fields in the table linked to the form.
- Forms may contain fields from more than one table.
- Any validation checks or controls put in place by the developer when they are creating the table will also be applied when data is entered using the form.
- The example below shows a form combining data from two tables. The main body of the form contains the member's personal details, while the sub-form contains data from the loan table.

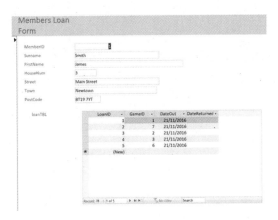

● Forms can contain navigational elements in the form of macros to help the user move between the various features of the database.

Queries

● Queries are used to extract data from a database. They can also be used to carry out additional processing on database content.

● Queries can be simple, using one table and a single search criteria, like this one:

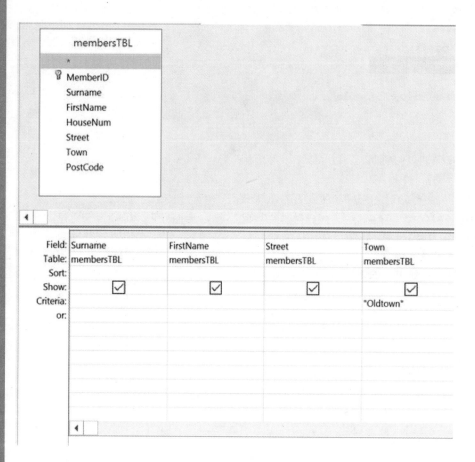

● Queries can be complex, using more than one table, perhaps including calculated fields or more than one search criteria. The following show examples of complex queries:

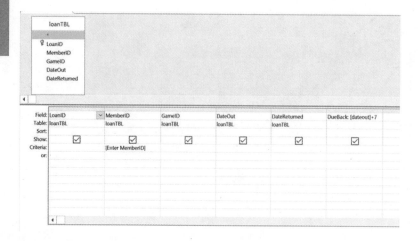

Example 1 shows the due back date is a calculated field entry

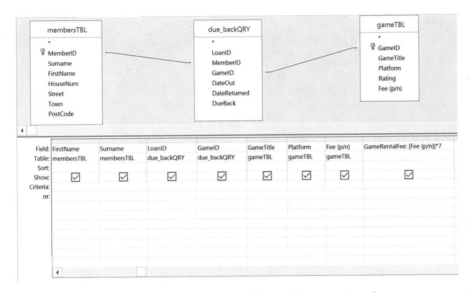

Example 2 shows how more than one table and the results of a query can be used to create a more complex query

SQL

- Some developers use **SQL** to extract data from relational databases.
- SQL statements have three main components:
  - select: to specify what data is to be displayed
  - from: to identify the source of the data to be interrogated
  - where: to identify the criteria to be used to select data from the source.
- The following examples show how we could use SQL to extract data from our GameLibrary database.
  - To select all members in membersTBL who lived in Oldtown and only display their Surname, First Name and Town:

SQL query	Result
SELECT membersTBL.[Surname], membersTBL. [FirstName], membersTBL.[Town] FROM membersTBL WHERE (((membersTBL.[Town])="Oldtown"));	Jones, Amy, Oldtown Brown, Jack, Oldtown

  - To select all members in membersTBL who lived in High Street in Oldtown and only display their Surname, First Name, Street and Town:

SQL query	Result
SELECT membersTBL.[Surname], membersTBL.[FirstName], membersTBL.[Street], membersTBL.[Town] FROM membersTBL WHERE (((membersTBL.Street)="High Street") AND ((membersTBL.Town)="Oldtown"));	Jones, Amy, High Street, Oldtown

Reports for data presentation

- Database applications use reports to display information to users in a user-friendly and professional manner.
- Reports can be generated from the contents of tables or queries and can combine data from more than one table or more than one query.
- Some reports may include additional processing, such as further grouping of data, sorting of data or, in more complex examples, it is possible for reports to contain fields where the data is calculated using the contents of other fields in the report.

Customer Receipt

Member ID	FirstName	Surname				
1	James	Smith				

GameID	LoanID	GameTitle	Platform	Fee (p/n)	Game Rental Fee
3	4	RatchetPlant	PC	£4.00	£28.00
6	5	Lego Jurassic World	PC	£2.00	£14.00
				Total Fee Due:	£42.00

GameID	LoanID	GameTitle	Platform	Fee (p/n)	Game Rental Fee
1	1	FIFA 17	Xbox OneS	£2.00	£14.00
2	3	Football Manager	Xbox OneS	£2.00	£14.00
7	2	Minecraft	Xbox OneS	£3.00	£21.00
				Total Fee Due:	£49.00
				Overall Total:	£91.00

A complex report with calculated fields (Total Fee Due and Overall Total) and data grouped by Platform

Macros for task automation

- Macros are small programs written to allow the user to automatically complete repetitive tasks.
- In a database application, macros can be added to forms and reports to help the user with both task completion and navigation.

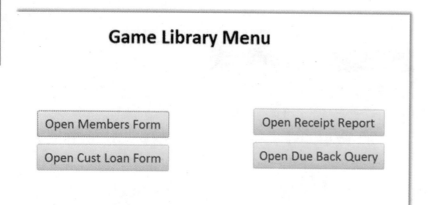

Example 1 shows a form with macro buttons being used as a main menu for users

Now test yourself answers and glossary at www.hoddereducation.co.uk/myrevisionnotes

Customer Receipt				Main Menu	Print Receipt

Member ID	FirstName	Surname			
1	James	Smith			

GameID	LoanID	GameTitle	Platform	Fee (p/n)	Game Rental Fee
3	4	RatchetPlant	PC	£4.00	£28.00
6	5	Lego Jurassic World	PC	£2.00	£14.00
			Total Fee Due:		£42.00

Example 2 shows a report document that includes macro buttons for printing and for navigation

Mail merge

- Mail merge is a process used to create personalised documents using a word-processed document containing a combination of fields inserted from a database file and fixed text that will appear for all recipients of the document.
- Data can be inserted into the mail merge document using queries or tables, which exist in the source database. The stages in completing a mail merge include:
  - creating the word-processed document to be sent to the recipients
  - creating a link between the word-processed document and the data source
  - inserting the relevant fields into the word-processed document
  - merging the word-processed document and the database contents.

Common mistakes

- Forms and reports and the roles they play in database applications can often be confused; remember that forms are used for data input and reports are used for output.
- Remember during database development that any attributes where the values are to be calculated should not be stored as permanent data items in the database, but instead should be calculated at the time of output. This helps to reduce the size of the database file.

Exam tip

It is important that you remember all of the practical skills you developed while completing your controlled assessment tasks. Any of these skills could be called upon to answer a question in your written examination.

Now test yourself

1 Explain the term 'data redundancy'. [2 marks]
2 Explain the term 'data integrity'. [2 marks]
3 List the three different types of relationship that can be created between tables in a relational database. [3 marks]
4 Some tables in a relational database contain foreign key fields. Explain the term 'foreign key field'. [3 marks]
5 Write the formula used to produce the results for Total Fee Due and Overall Fee Payable in the report shown below. [4 marks]

Customer Receipt

Main Menu   Print Receipt

Member ID	FirstName	Surname
1	James	Smith

GameID	LoanID	GameTitle	Platform	Fee (p/n)	Game Rental Fee
3	4	RatchetPlant	PC	£4.00	£28.00
6	5	Lego Jurassic World	PC	£2.00	£14.00
				Total Fee Due:	£42.00

Revision activity

- Research the term 'enforce referential integrity'. How does enforcing referential integrity help improve data integrity?
- Select a form used by someone at home to join a gym or some other club and create an appropriate database table(s) to store the data held in the form. Pay particular attention to data types, field sizes, any validation methods and input masks you could use to minimise data entry. Consider how the data could potentially be stored on more than one table in a relational database. Plan or implement any queries (simple and complex) you could create using the data stored in the database and therefore any reports that might be generated using the data in the database. Pay particular attention to where you might need to include calculated fields in any reports you are creating.

17 Significance of testing and developing appropriate test plans

The development process

Different approaches can be taken to the development of a new digital application. Two of the more common approaches are:

- the **waterfall model**
- the **iterative development approach** (presented by various types of prototyping – see Chapter 12 for more detail on prototyping).

Waterfall model

- A sequential approach to system development:

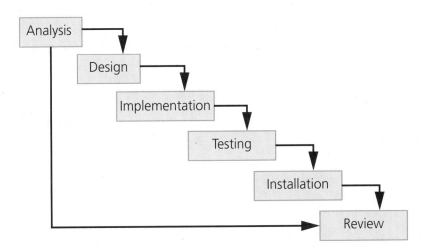

- Each stage must be completed in a fixed sequence.
- Each stage must be completed before the next can be embarked upon.

> **Waterfall model** A sequential approach to application development. A series of stages need to be completed in a fixed order, and each stage must be completed before the next one can begin
>
> **Iterative development approach** A step-by-step approach taken to the development of an application. Each step sees the life-cycle of analysis, design, development, testing, installation and review being repeated, each time adding more and more to the application until it is eventually completed

Iterative development process

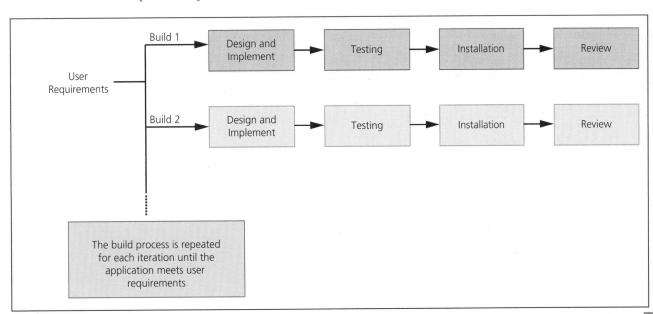

- Larger projects are broken down into smaller more manageable tasks.
- Each iteration undergoes its own development life cycle.
- Changes to the development of the application are built into the next iteration of the application.
- The completed solution evolves with each iteration as new features are added.
- A review is carried out at the end of each iteration so that errors are caught early in the development stages.

Responsibilities of the system tester

- Often the group of people responsible for testing an application is different from those who develop it. During testing, the focus should be on:
  - ensuring all user requirements were considered during the development process
  - detecting and fully documenting details of **bugs** encountered during the development process – documentation should include details of where the bug was encountered, steps leading up to the bug and any messages encountered (screenshots should be added to the documentation)
  - reporting bugs to the development team for correction.

> **System testing** Carried out on a complete and fully integrated system to ensure correct outputs are produced in compliance with the user requirements document
>
> **Bug** Another word for error or fault, which leads to errors in the execution of a program or an application

> **Exam tip**
>
> Ensure you have a clear understanding of the role of a system tester and the contents of any documentation they may produce.

The role of testing during the development process

REVISED

- User requirements can be mandatory or desirable. Testing not only helps determine whether all mandatory user requirements are met by the completed application; it also helps ensure errors are identified and helps the developer assess the reliability of the application.
  - During the waterfall model, testing takes place only once the entire system is developed. Errors detected at this stage can be difficult to rectify. It is important in the waterfall model that an effective design document is produced to help ensure all mandatory user requirements have been met.
  - During the iterative development approach, testing is carried out throughout the development process, so errors can be detected and corrected at an early stage and at a reduced cost and effort.
- An **effective test plan** includes:
  - an introductory section including details of the application
  - details of the testing approaches to be taken
  - a test strategy
  - examples of test data, including valid, invalid, **null** and **extreme** data
  - expected outcomes from the test
  - actual outcomes from the test
  - commentary on the outcomes or any corrections made afterwards.

> **Null data** Used to test that the system can cope when no data is entered
>
> **Extreme data** Used to test that the system can cope with very large or very small data values

Test no.	Area to be tested	Test data	Expected outcome	Test results	Corrections/ comments
3	Surname field	Null data: leave field blank	Field is a required data item: user should not be able to leave it blank	User cannot move on to add another record, but no feedback provided to explain error	Provide feedback to user explaining error which has occurred and how to correct it

Part of an example test strategy

Testing approaches

Approach to testing	Description
Black box testing	• The underlying design of the application being tested is unknown to the person carrying out the tests. • Test data is developed based around user requirements. • The aim is to identify errors relating to what the application is meant to do, not how it does it. • It is often carried out by someone not involved in the development of the application.
White box testing	• The underlying design of the application being tested is known to the tester. • It is generally carried out by those involved in the development of the software. • It may involve the use of **trace tables** to **dry-run** code. • It concentrates on testing application code and other underlying structures of the application.
System testing	• It can only be carried out when all individual components of the application have been fully developed and tested. • It ensures all individual components work together correctly. • No knowledge of the underlying constructs of the application is required.
Alpha and beta testing	• A small number of users not previously involved in the development normally carry out alpha testing. • Alpha testing is normally carried out on incomplete versions of an application, with the aim of detecting bugs in the application. • Beta testing is normally carried out just before the final version of an application is released commercially. • In beta testing, selected members of the target audience may be offered free trial versions of the application to use so that any remaining minor errors can be detected prior to the commercial release of the application.
A/B testing	• This is sometimes known as 'split testing'. • More than one version of an application is released (each to separate members of the target audience). • Statistical analysis is carried out to analyse the performance of the impact of one version of the application over the other.

Black box testing Where the tester is unaware of the internal structure of the application they are testing

White box testing A method of testing which examines the underlying structure of the application or code which has been developed

Trace table Created during a dry run containing all data items and output used in the section of code being reviewed. The value of each data item is documented after each line of the solution is executed

Dry run A paper-based exercise that allows the programmer to go through the solution step by step; the dry run will highlight any errors in the logic of the solution

Alpha testing Involves simulating the real-world environment the application has been designed for; normally carried out by a small number of users and prior to beta testing

Beta testing Carried out just after alpha testing and before the final version of the application is released commercially

A/B testing End users are presented with different versions of a digital application; statistical analysis is carried out to determine which is most successful

Multimedia testing

- Multimedia applications must be fully tested before commercial release. This helps ensure a positive experience for the end user and helps promote a professional image of the organisation.
- Some areas to focus on during the testing of a multimedia application include:
  - Navigation: it is important to ensure all internal and external hyperlinks remain live following the publication of the application.
  - The operation of multimedia assets: testing should ensure that all multimedia assets are in an optimised format, that they load correctly on all platforms and that appropriate plugins are available where necessary.
  - Load times: application testers should evaluate the load times for applications and individual pages on all target platforms.
  - Scripted and interactive elements: when testing these elements the testing team should ensure that all scripted elements are error free and that, if necessary, appropriate error codes are provided to support the end users' continued use of the application in the event of failure due to unavailability of plugin elements, for example.

> **Exam tip**
>
> Be able to look at a design document or a screenshot of a database or a multimedia application and design or describe appropriate tests one would expect to see in an effective test plan for that area of the application.

Now test yourself

TESTED

1 List three main steps of the waterfall development model. [3 marks]
2 Describe the iterative development process. [3 marks]
3 Explain how testing during the waterfall model differs from testing during the iterative development process. [2 marks]
4 List two key responsibilities of a system tester. [2 marks]
5 Explain the differences between testing during the waterfall model and the interactive development approach. [2 marks]
6 List two different types of test data you would expect to see in an effective test plan. [2 marks]
7 Explain the terms 'alpha' and 'beta' testing. [4 marks]
8 Describe the following methods of testing:
  (a) white box testing [2 marks]
  (b) black box testing [2 marks]
  (c) system testing. [2 marks]
9 List three key features one would expect to test in a multimedia digital application. [3 marks]

> **Revision activity**
>
> - Learn the definitions for each of the key words identified in this chapter.
> - Use the following terms to write a summary of no more than 100 words on the approaches to testing used by software developers: system testing, alpha testing, beta testing, white box testing, black box testing, A/B testing.
> - Copy out and learn the diagrams that illustrate the waterfall model and the iterative development process. Write a short paragraph about each in your own words.
> - Learn the features of an effective test plan.
> - Create a list of the main features to include in a test plan for a multimedia application.

> **Common mistake**
>
> Remember that testing can take place at various stages in the development of an application (depending on the approach taken to development).

18 Evaluation of digitally authored systems

Evaluation

- An **evaluation** is a document that considers the success of a project. Among other things, it will consider how complete the solution is, how efficient it is, how well it meets end user requirements and how well it operates on specified platforms.
- Evaluations should be carried out throughout the development of a system:
  - During the design stages: information gained here enables changes to be made without much cost.
  - During testing: test data helps identify problem areas within the solution to help ensure the solution operates correctly.

> **Evaluation** A document which considers the success of a project in relation to how complete the solution is, how efficient it is, how well it meets the end user's requirements and how well it operates on specified platforms

Who is involved in the evaluation process?

- The evaluation process can involve a wide range of groups or individuals, including:
  - members of the development team
  - management from the client organisation
  - end users.

Evidencing an evaluation

- An evaluation document should include the following details:
  - the purpose of the evaluation
  - the date, time and expected duration of the evaluation process
  - details of previous evaluations
  - lists of individuals involved in the evaluation process and the role they played
  - the stage at which the evaluation was carried out.
- Commentary should be included on:
  - why certain design decisions were made
  - **system robustness**, for example how effective user feedback was
  - system performance, for example whether the system generates incorrect results
  - details of possible improvements made to the solution
  - details of any deviations made from the original design
  - strengths and weaknesses of the system
  - performance of the development team in terms of time management, budget management and team contribution
  - areas for future development, based on end user feedback.
- Evidence to support findings should be presented in the form of:
  - design documents
  - documented results from testing

> **Robust system** A system can be considered to be robust if it does not crash when processing high levels of valid, invalid or exceptional data

○ questionnaires or interviews involving end users

○ reports on observations of the end users interacting with the application

○ results from user acceptance testing.

Common mistakes

It is a mistake to:

● consider evaluation from a personal point of view rather than in relation to user requirements: a good user evaluation must always take into consideration how well the developed solution has met the user requirements

● assume that evaluations are only carried out at the end of the development process: evaluations carried out throughout the development phases allow changes to be made to the solution at an early stage; this can help save money, as changes made at later stages in the development process can be costly to implement

● refer to the user requirements as the only evidence of a product evaluation: remember that evidence to support an evaluation can be collected from other stages in the product development cycle; some sources of evidence include design documents, results from testing, interview transcripts, questionnaires and observations.

Points to consider

REVISED

● A key element of any evaluation document is how well the solution meets the **qualitative** and **quantitative user requirements** of the application.

● Qualitative user requirements refer to the quality of the solution and can therefore be more subjective, while quantitative user requirements are more easily measured.

● Results based on user requirements can be presented as shown in this extract from an evaluation report:

> **Qualitative user requirements** Relate to the quality of the solution, and may be subjectively assessed, i.e. not everyone may assess them equally
>
> **Quantitative user requirements** Requirements which can be easily measured, for example in terms of time

User requirement number	Requirement	Evaluation findings	Actions taken/required
1	Provide a form to allow the user to enter new member details.	This form was easy to set up. The development team created a form that linked to the company database. The end user thought the form would look better if the company logo was included.	Add company logo to the form.
...	...	...	...
15	Results of a product search should be returned within 5 seconds.	The results were returned in less than 5 seconds for all searches carried out.	No action required.
...	...	...	...
27	The application should work on Android and iPhones as well as a range of web browsers on a PC.	All users reported the app worked well on all platforms.	No action required.

- A good evaluation will also:
  - be objective and include commentary on the strengths and weaknesses of the solution
  - identify areas where further modification is required
  - highlight if a full or partial solution has been met
  - consider the robustness of the solution
  - determine how close the solution is to the original design specification
  - consider the efficiency of the solution
  - consider how well the solution works on the platforms specified by the end user
  - include any commentary from those involved in the evaluation process.

Evaluating a database solution

- Alongside ensuring user requirements are met, the following should also be considered when evaluating a database solution:
  - Consistency of presentation, for example: do all on-screen and printed outputs have a similar layout, is navigation presented consistently across the package and do they all appear appropriately?
  - Is the package user friendly and intuitive?
  - Measures in place to help ensure data integrity, for example: Are appropriate validation and control methods in place?
  - Has data redundancy been removed from the application (through the removal of any many-to-many relationships)?
  - Has a consistent naming convention been applied to all database objects?
  - Are all repetitive tasks automated for ease of use?
  - Are all the results of processing presented effectively?

Evaluating a multimedia solution

- Alongside ensuring the user requirements have been met, the following should also be considered when evaluating a multimedia solution:
  - What design choices have been made following A/B testing (if applicable)?
  - Is the content balanced with appropriate use of white space and spacing of digital assets?
  - Is all content appropriate and of value to the end user?
  - Is the application easy to use, i.e. is the package user friendly and intuitive?
  - Are all screens consistent in terms of presentation of repeated content, such as navigation elements and headings?
  - Do all hyperlinks within the application function appropriately?
  - Do all pages within the application load within an appropriate time frame?
  - Are all digital assets in an appropriate (compressed) format and are they fully operational?
  - Do interactive elements function appropriately and is feedback (where provided) instant, appropriate and informative?

○ Is the application cross-platform compatible?

○ Is the application accessible to all members of the target audience?

● Any actions taken following the results of the evaluation process should be documented and included in the evaluation document.

Now test yourself

TESTED

1 List three items that should form part of a completed evaluation document. [3 marks]

2 Evidence must be provided to support conclusions drawn during the evaluation process. List three sources of evidence that can be included or referred to in an evaluation document. [3 marks]

3 Explain the purpose of an evaluation document. [2 marks]

4 User requirements form a key part of the evaluation. Use examples to explain the difference between qualitative and quantitative user requirements. [4 marks]

5 Evaluations can help the developer determine how robust their solution is. Explain the term 'robust' in this context. [2 marks]

Revision activity

● Learn definitions of each of the key words identified in this chapter.
● Summarise this topic using 100 words.

19 Contemporary trends in software development

Programming paradigms

REVISED

- A program is a set of instructions that tells a computer what to do in order to solve a particular problem.
- There are two main approaches to programming. These are called 'programming paradigms'. The two paradigms to be studied in the specification are the **procedural paradigm** and the **object-oriented paradigm**.

Procedural programming

- Procedural programming languages provide features to help programmers design solutions using a top-down approach. Top-down design involves breaking a complex problem into smaller sub-problems. Solutions for each sub-problem can be created and the code for the solutions can be written as functions (also called 'procedures' or **methods**).
- A program is made up of a number of functions that can be called repeatedly. Examples of procedural programming languages are C, COBOL and FORTRAN.
- Below is an example of a program that takes a number as input and outputs the cubed value of the number. The function 'cubed' is called and the value to be cubed is passed as a parameter to the function. The function returns the cubed value of the number input.

> **Procedural paradigm**
> An approach to developing a solution where the program operates on data and is organised in self-contained blocks called 'procedures'; the logic of the program is actioned by calling the procedures
>
> **Object-oriented paradigm**
> An approach to developing a solution where the focus is on data rather than processes; the data and the methods (program code) that operate on the data are contained within a single object class

> **Exam tip**
>
> Ensure you can describe the two programming paradigms and their particular features.

> **Methods** The behaviours that an object can perform, e.g. an object may have a method that prints all of the data contained within it onto the screen

```
cubed.cs  ↔ ×
ConsoleApplication1.Program
 1  using System;
 2  using System.Collections.Generic;
 3  using System.Linq;
 4  using System.Text;
 5  using System.Threading.Tasks;
 6
 7  namespace ConsoleApplication1
 8  {
 9      class Program
10      {
11          static void Main(string[] args)
12          {
13              //variables or data to be sed in the program are declared below
14              int value, cubedValue;
15
16              Console.WriteLine("Enter a number to calculate cubed value ");
17              value = Convert.ToInt32(Console.ReadLine());
18
19              //The function (or method) is called in the line below
20              cubedValue = cubed(value);
21
22              Console.WriteLine("The cubed value of " + value + " is " + cubedValue);
23              Console.ReadLine();
24
25          }
26
27
28          static int cubed(int x)//function (or method) definition
29          {
30              int p = x * x * x;
31              return p;
32
33          }
34      }
35  }
36
```

Object-oriented programming

- Object-oriented programming languages provide features to help programmers design solutions using **objects**.

- Objects contain both the data (known as **properties**) and the functions (known as 'methods') to be used in the solution.

- A class is like a template or blueprint for an object; it defines the properties and methods for a group of objects.

- **Inheritance** allows programmers to build one class based on another class, i.e. one class can inherit the characteristics of another parent class (also called 'superclass' or 'base class'). In this derived class (also called 'subclass') only the differences between it and the parent class need to be coded.

- **Encapsulation** 'hides' the data belonging to an object. The data can only be accessed through the methods associated with the object. Therefore the object-oriented approach creates more efficient reusable code.

- Advantages of object-oriented programming are:

  o The code for an object can be programmed and maintained independently.

  o The code for an object can be re-used in different programs by different developers.

  o The details of an object's internal implementation are hidden from the outside world, so direct access to the object's data is reduced.

- Here is a simple example of a class, created using C#.

- The class name is Shape.

- A shape has two attributes or pieces of data: shapename and colour.

- The class Shape has one method called Describe. This method will print the colour and shapename for an object of the class Shape.

- The properties ShapeName and Colour allow the data within the class to be accessed.

> **Object** A self-contained element that contains the properties and methods needed to access and manipulate data values
>
> **Properties** Contain code that facilitates reading and writing to the data within an object
>
> **Inheritance** Enables the properties of one class to be copied to another so that only the differences between the classes need to be reprogrammed
>
> **Encapsulation** Hides an object's data so that it can only be directly accessed by the methods within the object

Common mistakes

Do not confuse inheritance and encapsulation. Be sure to learn the correct definition for each.

```
Program.cs  ⇔ ×
ConsoleApplication1.Shape
 7  ⊟namespace ConsoleApplication1
 8   {
 9  ⊟    class Program
10       {
11  ⊟        static void Main(string[] args)
12           {
13               Shape shape;
14
15               shape = new Shape("Red", "Circle");
16               Console.WriteLine(shape.Describe());
17
18               shape = new Shape("Green","Square");
19               Console.WriteLine(shape.Describe());
20
21               Console.ReadLine();
22
23           }
24       }
25
26  ⊟    class Shape
27       {
28           private string shapename;
29           private string colour;
30
31  ⊟        public Shape(string colour, string shapename)
32           {
33               this.colour = colour;
34               this.shapename = shapename;
35           }
36
37  ⊟        public string Describe()
38           {
39               return "This is a " + Colour + " " + ShapeName + "." ;
40           }
41
42  ⊟        public string ShapeName
43           {
44               get { return shapename; }
45               set { shapename = value; }
46           }
47  ⊟        public string Colour
48           {
49               get { return colour; }
50               set { colour = value; }
51           }
52       }
53   }
54
```

Now test yourself answers and glossary at www.hoddereducation.co.uk/myrevisionnotes

- The main program defines objects of the class Shape; in the first instance a Red Circle and in the second a Green Square.
- When the program is executed the following is shown on the screen:

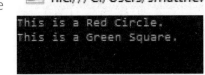

Software development environments

- Although code can be written in a simple text editor, most programmers now use a **software development environment** (also known as an 'integrated development environment'). The tools provided include:
  - an editing window that allows the programmer to enter and edit code; it also provides access to objects, methods, properties and events at design time
  - a clipboard, used to copy and paste
  - colour, used throughout the coding window to aid readability for the programmer; the editor may use different colours for keywords and **syntax errors** may also be colour coded
  - collapsible code sections: programmers can collapse/expand selected sections of code to make viewing large programs much easier
  - line numbering, used to help programmers to distinguish between lines in long programs; line numbers are also used by the compiler to reference the location of errors in the code
  - code completion tools: when writing code there is instant, automatic, context-sensitive help; as a statement is entered, its full syntax may be shown to the programmer – the code completion tool may provide a list of available functions, statements, constants or values that the programmer can choose from.

High-level code translation and execution

- Program code must be translated into **machine code** so that the computer can understand and execute the instructions.
- The program written by the programmer is called the **source code** and the translated version of the program is called the 'object code'.
- A language compiler is built in to the software development environment. It processes each statement in the source code and tries to translate the whole program into machine code, before executing it.
- The compiler will perform a number of passes on the code:
  - The first pass will involve checking the syntax of each statement. If the syntax is not correct, the program will not be executed. The programmer must correct the errors before attempting to compile the program again.
  - If the program uses libraries, the compiler will include the library code used in the program; this is called pre-processing. In C# programs, pre-processor directives are preceded by the '#' symbol, for example #define.
  - During lexical analysis the compiler converts source code into fixed-length binary code items called 'tokens and parsing' (or 'syntax analysis'), which checks that the statements conform to the rules of grammar for the language.
  - Semantic analysis ensures that any variables used have been declared and data types are correctly matched.

Software development environment Software that provides programmers with an integrated set of programming tools to build an application from coding through to testing

Syntax errors An error in the code entered into the code editor, e.g. a misspelling or the omission of a symbol

Exam tip

You should be familiar with the features provided by a software development environment and be able to explain the process of high-level code translation and program execution.

Machine code Instructions in binary format that can be executed directly by the computer

Source code The original program code written by the programmer

19 Contemporary trends in software development

o The optimised machine code version of the source code is generated and can be executed.

o Executing, or 'running', a program means that the machine code instructions are loaded into memory and the computer performs the instructions. These instructions cause simple actions in the computer.

Now test yourself

1 Describe how procedural and object-oriented programming approaches differ. [4 marks]
2 List the characteristics of a good software development environment. [3 marks]
3 Describe the process of high-level language translation and explain why it is required. [6 marks]

Revision activity

- Learn the features of the procedural and object-oriented approaches to programming and the advantages of object-oriented programming.
- Review the software development environment that you use and identify the features it provides you with for creating software.
- Review some of your coding examples and compile them. Observe the compilation (or high-level language translation) process. Record syntax errors and note how you fixed these errors.
- Learn the steps involved in the translation of high-level code.

20 Digital data

Converting numbers into binary patterns

- See Chapter 1 for binary digits and **ASCII code**.
- Data must be converted to binary format so that it can be stored and understood by computers. There are a number of methods for doing this.

Understanding place values

- The number 147_{10} is equal to one hundred, four tens and seven units.

T	H	T	U
1000 (10^3)	100 (10^2)	10 (10^1)	1 (10^0)
	1	4	7

> **ASCII code** Acronym for the American Standard Code for Information Interchange; ASCII is a code for representing English characters as numbers – each letter is assigned a number from 0 to 127, for example the ASCII code for the letter A is 65

- $(1 \times 10^2) + (4 \times 10^1) + (7 \times 10^0) = 147$ or $(1 \times 100) + (4 \times 10) + (7 \times 1) = 147$
- Binary digits also have place values. In the binary system, place values are based on powers of 2, as shown.

128	64	32	16	8	4	2	1
2^7	2^6	2^5	2^4	2^3	2^2	2^1	2^0
1	0	0	1	0	0	1	1

- So, the binary pattern 10010011 is equivalent to the denary number 147:
  $(1 \times 2^7) + (1 \times 2^4) + (1 \times 2^1) + (1 \times 2^0) = 147$ or $(1 \times 128) + (1 \times 16) + (1 \times 2) + (1 \times 1) = 147$

Using divide by two to convert from denary to binary

- The resulting binary pattern is created by copying the bit values from the bottom up.
  10010011

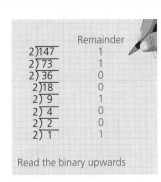

Read the binary upwards

Using divide by two

Using place value to create the binary number pattern

- Consider $147_{10.}$ To use place value, write down the place values of each power of two.
- Go to the highest value and check to see if that value can be taken away from 147. If so, put a 1 beside the value. The table on the next page shows how to continue.

> **Common mistakes**
>
> Entering bits in the incorrect column results in the incorrect place value.
>
> Ensure you copy the bit pattern generated from the 'divide by two method' in the correct order (it should be bottom up).

Using 147:

128 (2^7)	1	Can 128 be taken away from 147? Yes: 147 − 128 = 19
64 (2^6)	0	Can 64 be taken away from 19? No.
32 (2^5)	0	Can 32 be taken away from 19? No.
16 (2^4)	1	Can 16 be taken away from 19? Yes: 19 − 16 = 3
8 (2^3)	0	Can 8 be taken away from 3? No.
4 (2^2)	0	Can 4 be taken away from 3? No.
2 (2^1)	1	Can 2 be taken away from 3? Yes: 3 − 2 = 1
1 (2^0)	1	Can 1 be taken away from 1? Yes: 1 − 1 = 0

- Again, giving the binary pattern 10010011, which represents the denary value 147. There are 8 bits in this sequence. 8 bits is equivalent to 1 byte.

Binary coded decimal (BCD)

- Each decimal digit is represented by a group of 4 binary digits, for example 147:

1	4	7
0001	0100	0111

- So, 147_{10} = 000101000111 in BCD.

Character representation

REVISED

ASCII code

- The original **7-bit ASCII code table** used seven bits to represent text and there were 128 characters in the table. These characters include the letters A to Z and other common characters.
- The **8-bit ASCII table** contains 256 characters ($2^8 = 256$); it makes use of the 8th bit in a byte. The characters in the 8-bit ASCII table include all those in the 7-bit table and regional characters and symbols, for example, the Microsoft® Windows Latin-1 extended characters.
- The 8-bit ASCII table, however, was limited and could only represent 256 characters. This means languages with many more characters could not be represented fully. Also, the characters numbered 128 to 255 were used differently for different regions, leading to incompatibility between character sets.

7-bit ASCII table Also known as Standard ASCII, uses 7 bits to represent each character; only 128 characters could be represented in the character set

8-bit ASCII table Also known as Extended ASCII, uses 8 bits to represent each character; a further 128 characters can be represented in the character set, totalling 256 characters

Unicode

- **Unicode** is a character-encoding standard created to solve the problem of the limitations of ASCII code.
- Unicode provides a unique number for every character as the current Unicode set contains over 100 000 characters.
- All ASCII characters are part of Unicode and they have the same numbers as in the ASCII character set.
- Characters are called 'code points'.

Unicode A standard for encoding characters, Unicode typically uses 16 bits to represent a character and so can represent up to 65 000 characters

- There are a number of encoding methods:
  - UTF-32: fixed length encoding using 32 bits regardless of the character. This is inefficient when compared to ASCII, which represents a character in 1 byte.
  - UTF-8: a variable-length encoding system that uses one byte for the common characters. ASCII character codes are unchanged so ASCII text is also UTF-8. Some other characters are encoded with two or more bytes. This typing of encoding is backward compatible with ASCII coding.
  - UTF-16: a variable-length encoding system that uses a minimum of 2-byte number units per character.

Using binary, decimal and hexadecimal number systems

REVISED ☐

Hexadecimal number representation

- **Hexadecimal**, or hex, is a numbering system that uses the base 16. Hexadecimal values are expressed as the digits 0–9 and the letters A–F, giving sixteen possibilities.

> **Hexadecimal** A numbering system that uses the base 16

Hexadecimal number	0	1	2	3	4	5	6	7	8	9	A	B	C	D	E	F
Equivalent decimal number	0	1	2	3	4	5	6	7	8	9	10	11	12	13	14	15

- Hexadecimal can be used to simplify long binary patterns. One hexadecimal digit can represent a group of 4 bits. If you want to look at a 64-bit memory address you can look at the 64-bit number pattern or the 16-digit hexadecimal pattern, for example, the 16-bit pattern:

1001 0110   1000   1011   becomes:

9   6   8   B   in hexadecimal.

- Place values in hexadecimal are arranged similarly to those in the denary and binary numbering systems.

65536	4096	256	16	1
16^4	16^3	16^2	16^1	16^0
			1	1

- The number shown above $11_h = 17_{10}$, i.e. $(1 \times 16^1) + (1 \times 16^0) = 16 + 1 = 17$
- Hexadecimal is used to represent colour codes on computers. The three primary colours (red, green and blue) have two-digit hexadecimal codes, ranging from 00 to FF (0 to 255 in decimal). These are placed together to form a six-digit hexadecimal code.

Converting between denary, binary and hexadecimal

- To convert the binary pattern 1001 1011 to hexadecimal:

1	Split the binary pattern into 4-bit groups	1001	1011
2	Establish the denary value for each group	$(8+1=9_{10}=9_{16})$	$(8+2+1=11_{10}=B_{16})$
3	Convert from denary to hexadecimal	9	B
	Result	$9B_{16}$	

- To convert the hexadecimal pattern 9B to denary:

• Convert each hexadecimal value into its binary equivalent	9 B (hex) 1001 1011 (binary)
• Convert the binary number into denary	$(1 \times 128) + (0 \times 64) + (0 \times 32) + (1 \times 16) + (1 \times 8) + (0 \times 4) + (1 \times 2) + (1 \times 1)$ $= 128 + 16 + 8 + 2 + 1$
• Result	155_{10}

- Or, alternatively, use place values for the base 16:

  9B = 144 + 11 = 155

  i.e. $(9 \times 16) + (11 \times 1)$

Sign and magnitude and complementation

- These can be used to represent negative and positive numbers.
- The left-most bit is reserved for the sign and the rest of the binary pattern represents the size of the number, for example in 10000111 the left-most 1 represents the sign bit and the remaining 7 bits are the magnitude of the number. Therefore, the number is –7.
- Complementation is another way of representing positive and negative numbers. The left-most bit (most significant bit) indicates the sign of the binary pattern.
- **One's complement**: Each bit is inverted, so a 1 bit changes to a 0 bit and each 0 bit changes to a 1 bit.

  For example, +37 in binary is 00100101.

  Using one's complement: –37 = 11011010.

  For one's complement using 8 bits it is possible to represent the denary numbers –127 to +127.
- The **two's complement** of –37:
  1 Change the bit pattern to one's complement: 11011010.
  2 Add 1 to the resulting binary pattern: 11011010 + 1 = 11011011.
  3 The most significant bit (left-most) is now a 1, indicating a negative number (–37).

  Using 8 bits in two's complement, it is possible to represent the denary numbers –128 to +127.

One's complement Can be used to represent a binary number; when using one's complement, each bit is inverted, so a 1 bit changes to a 0 bit, and each 0 bit is changed to a 1 bit

Two's complement A method of representing signed numbers in a computer system

Adding two bytes together

- A binary digit can only take on values of 0 or 1, therefore a 'carry' is generated when two bits of value '1' are added. Consider the following example.

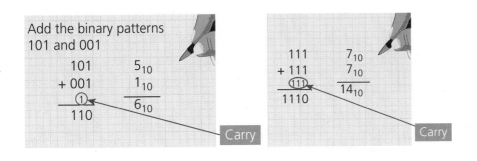

Add the binary patterns
101 and 001

$$101 \quad 5_{10}$$
$$+ \ 001 \quad 1_{10}$$
$$\underline{\quad ① \quad} \quad \underline{\quad 6_{10}}$$
$$110$$

Carry

$$111 \quad 7_{10}$$
$$+ \ 111 \quad 7_{10}$$
$$\underline{⑪⑴ \quad} \quad \underline{14_{10}}$$
$$1110$$

Carry

- Add the binary patterns 101 and 001.
- Adding the bits 1 + 1 gives 0 and a carry of 1.
- What about adding 111 to 111?
- Adding the bits 1 + 1 + 1 gives 1 and a carry of 1.

Carry	1		1		1		0	
			1		1		1	
+			1		1		1	
Result	**1**		**1**		**1**		**0**	

- The result is a 4-bit pattern.
- Bytes (8-bit patterns) are added together in the same way. The maximum number that can be represented in a byte (8-bit word) is 255_{10}. That is 11111111 ($128 + 64 + 32 + 16 + 8 + 4 + 2 + 1 = 255$). If the result of a calculation exceeds this number, an error will occur.

  For example: $129 + 129 = 258$.

Carry	1					1		
129	1	0	0	0	0	0	0	1
129 +	1	0	0	0	0	0	0	1
Result	**0**	**0**	**0**	**0**	**0**	**0**	**1**	**0**

- The result generated is (1) 00000010.

  The extra bit, in brackets, is known as **overflow**. Overflow occurs when the magnitude of the number is greater than the maximum number that can be represented by the computer; in this case 255. The left-most 1 cannot be stored and is lost, therefore the result generated by this addition is 2_{10}, which is incorrect.

> **Overflow** Occurs when the magnitude of the number is greater than the maximum number that can be represented by the computer

Negative calculations

- Calculate $48 - 24$. This is achieved by calculating $48 + (-24)$.

  Find -24 by converting the binary pattern for 24 to the two's complement form:

  $11100111 + 1 = 11101000$

Carry	1	1	1					
48	0	0	1	1	0	0	0	0
−24	1	1	1	0	1	0	0	0
Result 24	**0**	**0**	**0**	**1**	**1**	**0**	**0**	**0**

● Has overflow occurred?

  Examine the last two carry bits. If these are the same, overflow has not occurred and the result is correct. If the last two bits of the carry are different then overflow has occurred. In this case, overflow has not occurred and the result is correct. The 9th bit is ignored.

Exam tip

Ensure that you understand place values for binary and hexadecimal numbers. You must be able to convert from denary to binary to hexadecimal and vice versa. You must be able to add two bytes together and recognise whether or not overflow has occurred.

Truth tables

● Computers carry out logical operations and apply logical (or Boolean) operators such as AND, NOT and OR to Boolean variables. A Boolean variable can take only one of two values: 1 or 0 (true or false).

NOT operator

● The NOT operator has one input. The truth table for the NOT operator is shown to the right.

X	NOT X
0	1
1	0

AND operator

● The AND operator can have any number of inputs. All inputs must be equal to 1 or true for an overall output of 1 or true to be obtained. The truth table for the AND operator is shown to the right using a 2-bit input sequence.

X	Y	X AND Y
0	0	0
0	1	0
1	0	0
1	1	1

OR operator

● The OR operator can have any number of inputs. At least one input must be equal to 1 or true for an overall output of 1 or true to be obtained. The truth table for the OR operator is shown to the right using a 2-bit input sequence.

X	Y	X OR Y
0	0	0
0	1	1
1	0	1
1	1	1

XOR operator

● The XOR (exclusive OR) operator can have any number of inputs. An output of 1 will be obtained if only 1 (not all) of the input values is equal to 1. The truth table for the XOR operator is shown to the right using a 2-bit input sequence.

● This type of logic is used in programming during selection, when parts of the program will be executed based on evaluating a Boolean expression, for example if A = 4 and B = 6 and C = 10 which of the following statements will be output?

X	Y	X OR Y
0	0	0
0	1	1
1	0	1
1	1	0

```
IF (A>B and A>C)

OUTPUT "A is the largest value"

ELSE IF (B>A and B>C)

OUTPUT "B is the largest value"

ELSE

OUTPUT "C is the largest value"

END-IF
```

Answer: C is the largest value.

Using data types

- See Chapter 1 for descriptions of the following data types: numeric (integer and real), date/time, character and string.
- When developing a software application, all data used must be given a data type so that it can be stored and processed correctly as a binary pattern.
- This data or variable should be given a name that reflects its purpose in the program. Programming languages such as C# are strongly typed.
- Most programming languages have built-in data types that include data types for integers, strings and characters. Date/time values can be retrieved using special functions within the programming language. The program below makes use of all of these data types.

```csharp
DataTypes.Program                                          Main(string[] args)
 9      class Program
10      {
11          static void Main(string[] args)
12          {
13              //declare variables
14              DateTime today = new DateTime();
15              string studentName = "";
16              double courseWorkMark = 0.0;
17              double examMark = 0.0;
18              double totalMark;
19              char overallGrade = ' ';
20
21              Console.Write("Enter Student Name ");
22              studentName = Console.ReadLine();
23              Console.Write("Enter coursework mark ");
24              courseWorkMark = Convert.ToDouble(Console.ReadLine());
25              Console.Write("Enter exam mark ");
26              examMark = Convert.ToDouble(Console.ReadLine());
27
28              totalMark = examMark + courseWorkMark;
29
30              if (totalMark > 75)
31                  overallGrade = 'A';
32              else if (totalMark > 65)
33                  overallGrade = 'B';
34              else if (totalMark > 55)
35                  overallGrade = 'C';
36              else overallGrade = 'D';
37
38              Console.WriteLine("Student " + studentName + " has achieved an overall mark of " + totalMark);
39              Console.WriteLine(" This is a Grade " + overallGrade + ".  This has been achieved on " + today.DayOfWeek.ToString() +".");
40              Console.ReadKey();
41
42          }
43      }
44  }
45
```

C# program, which uses different data types

```
Enter Student Name Anthony
Enter coursework mark 44
Enter exam mark 45
Student Anthony has achieved an overall mark of 89
 This is a Grade A.  This has been achieved on Monday.
```

Output from the program shown above

Now test yourself

1 Convert the following numbers to binary patterns: 23, 53, 100, 64. [4 marks]
2 Evaluate ASCII code and Unicode as character-encoding standards. [6 marks]
3 Describe how negative numbers can be represented in binary patterns. [4 marks]
4 Perform the following calculations using 8-bit binary addition and determine whether or not overflow has occurred: 25 + 9, 100 + 28, 34 – 17, 88 + 50. [12 marks]
5 Copy and complete the table below by applying the Boolean operators shown. [6 marks]

A	B	C	D=NOT C	E= A AND D	F= D OR E
0	0	0			
0	0	1			
0	1	0			
0	1	1			
1	0	0			
1	0	1			
1	1	0			
1	1	1			

6 Describe the following data types and give examples of how each might be used to hold data in a programming language of your choice: integer, real, string, character. [12 marks]

Revision activity

- Learn a method for converting denary numbers to binary patterns.
- Review the 7-bit and 8-bit ASCII code tables and examine their character sets.
- Review a subset of the Unicode character set and explain why the Unicode standard was developed.
- Practise adding bytes together and check for overflow in each calculation.
- Practise applying the rules of logic for AND, OR and NOT.
- Learn descriptions and examples of the use of the different data types.

21 Digital design principles

The underlying concepts of computational thinking

REVISED

- The four key elements to computational thinking are:
  - **Decomposition**: involves breaking a large, complex problem into smaller sub-problems and then examining each sub-problem to provide a solution. The small solutions can be brought together to provide an overall solution to the complex problem.
  - **Pattern recognition**: involves observing key characteristics, patterns and trends in the data that is being considered.
  - **Abstraction**: involves removing specific details from a problem that are not needed to solve it.
  - **Algorithm**: used to design a solution. This is a step-by-step set of instructions that specifies how the problem is going to be solved. The order of the instructions in an algorithm is important. Both **flowcharts** and **pseudo-code** can be used in algorithm design.

> **Decomposition** Breaking a complex problem down into smaller, more manageable problems called sub-problems
>
> **Pattern recognition** Identifying patterns and trends in data
>
> **Abstraction** Filtering out details about the problem that will not be required for the solution

Using algorithms, flowcharts and pseudo-code

REVISED

- Flow diagrams and pseudo-code are methods of representing solutions to a problem.
- Pseudo-code is used to represent a solution to a problem. Pseudo-code makes use of keywords and control structures in a similar way to a programming language.
- A flow diagram or flowchart is a graphical representation of the solution to a problem. The flowchart uses special symbols to represent different operations, flow lines represent the sequence of operations and arrows on the flow lines represent the direction of flow from top to bottom or left to right.
- Some of the symbols used for flowcharts are shown below.

> **Algorithm** A set of step-by-step instructions representing the solution to a problem
>
> **Flowchart** A graphical representation that includes special symbols and flow lines to represent the solution to a problem
>
> **Pseudo-code** A set of English-like, language-independent instructions that uses keywords and control structures to represent the solution to a problem

Graphic	Symbol	Purpose
→	Flow line	Indicates the flow of logic and connects the different symbols together
(rounded rectangle)	Terminal (Stop/Start)	Represents the start and end of the flowchart
(parallelogram)	Input/Output	Indicates input or output of data

Graphic	Symbol	Purpose
	Process	Indicates that an operation is to be done. There is usually text in the rectangle
	Decision	Asks a question; there are a number of alternative answers and a pathway is selected based on the response to the question
	Sub-routine symbol	Represents a call to a sub-routine
	Document/Report	Indicates that a report or document is used or produced

● Consider the following problem. A program is required to take as input ten numbers representing student scores in an examination and calculate and output the average score. A flowchart representing a solution to this problem is shown.

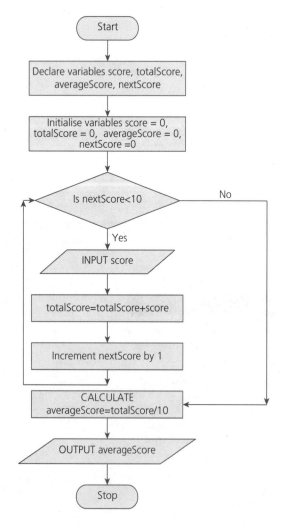

Flowchart showing how the average score is calculated

- Solutions can also be represented using pseudo-code. A solution for the above problem using pseudo-code is shown below.

```
Initialise score, totalScore, averageScore,
nextScore
WHILE nextScore is less than 10
    INPUT score
    totalScore = totalScore + score
    increment nextScore by 1
END WHILE
CALCULATE AVERAGE
OUTPUT averageScore
CALCULATE AVERAGE
averageScore=totalScore/10
```

Pseudo-code showing how the average score is calculated

Algorithms for sorting

- Sorting algorithms are used by computers to sort data. There are many different sorting algorithms and each can be evaluated in terms of:
  - the speed at which it sorts large amounts of data
  - the amount of memory used during the sorting process
  - the number of comparisons carried out within a sort
  - the number of exchanges carried out during a sort
  - the stability of the sort (a sorting algorithm is said to be stable if two objects with equal keys appear in the same order in sorted output as they appear in the input list to be sorted).
- Simple sorting algorithms include the **bubble sort** and the **insertion sort**.

> **Bubble sort** A simple sort method that repeatedly steps through a list of data items; adjacent elements are compared and swapped if they are in the wrong order
>
> **Insertion sort** A simple sorting algorithm that builds a sorted sub-list one item at a time; the sub-list becomes the new sorted list

The bubble sort and the insertion sort

- The table below shows how the bubble and insertion sorts differ with regard to the number of comparisons and the number of exchanges.

> **Exam tip**
>
> Ensure you understand both the bubble and insertion sorts. You should be able to recognise these and comment on the efficiency of sorting and searching methods.

Sort	Number of comparisons		Number of exchanges	
	Average Case	Worst Case	Average Case	Worst Case
Bubble Sort	$N^2/2$	$N^2/2$	$N^2/2$	$N^2/2$
Insertion Sort	$N^2/4$	$N^2/2$	$N^2/8$	$N^2/4$

- N= number of data items.
- A comparison is when two items of data are compared to each other.
- An exchange is when items of data swap their position in the list.
- The insertion sort can be more efficient than the bubble sort in terms of comparisons and exchanges.

Bubble sort	Insertion sort
• Inefficient for sorting large amounts of data – the time taken to sort data is related to the square of the number of items to be sorted • The algorithm works by swapping adjacent data items until they are in the correct order • Data items 'bubble' up through the list until they are in the correct order	• Adaptive – the performance adapts to the initial order of the elements; this algorithm may be used when the data items are nearly sorted • Stable – retains the relative order of the same elements • Requires a constant amount of memory as the entire sort occurs in internal memory

Storing data for sorting

- An array is used to store the data items to be sorted.
- An array is a data structure that holds a set of data items all of the same type. It is given a name and the data items or elements are accessed using the array name followed by their position in the array.
- Usually, an array is zero indexed, meaning that the first element can be accessed by giving the following details: Arrayname[0].

How does the bubble sort work?

- Imagine an array called myNumbers that has the following six integers stored: 47, 69, 12, 34, 25, 39.
- The data needs to be sorted using the bubble sort method.
- Adjacent elements are compared; if they are out of sequence, they swap positions.
- At the end of the first pass, the largest value is in the last position in the array (see below).
- This process is repeated. On the second pass, the second largest value is moved to the second last array position, and so on.
- The table below shows the results after one full pass through the array of data. Five comparisons are performed.

Comparison	my Numbers[0]	my Numbers[1]	my Numbers[2]	my Numbers[3]	my Numbers[4]	my Numbers[5]	Exchange
1	**47**	**69**	12	34	25	39	47 > 69? No No swap
2	47	**69**	**12**	34	25	39	69 > 12? Yes Swap
3	47	12	**69**	**34**	25	39	69 > 34? Yes Swap
4	47	12	34	**69**	**25**	39	69 > 25? Yes Swap
5	47	12	34	25	**69**	**39**	69 > 39? Yes Swap
	47	12	34	25	39	**69**	

Largest value in last position of array

How does the insertion sort work?

- Consider the same data in an insertion sort.
- The tables below show the results after one full pass using the insertion sort algorithm.
- Each comparison examines two adjacent elements in the array of data. When a data item is swapped it is added to the sorted sub-list in the correct order. At the end of one full pass, the array of data is fully sorted.

Com-parison	my Numbers[0]	my Numbers[1]	my Numbers[2]	my Numbers[3]	my Numbers[4]	my Numbers[5]	Exchange
1	**47**	**69**	12	34	25	39	47 > 69? No No change

Comp-arison	my Numbers[0]	my Numbers[1]	my Numbers[2]	my Numbers[3]	my Numbers[4]	my Numbers[5]	Exchange
2	**47**	**69**	**12**	34	25	39	69 > 12? Yes Swap and add to sorted sublist
3	**47**	**12**	69	34	25	39	check new sorted sublist. 47 > 12? Yes Swap
4	**12**	**47**	69	34	25	39	Note that the sorted sublist now contains two values

Comp-arison	my Numbers[0]	my Numbers[1]	my Numbers[2]	my Numbers[3]	my Numbers[4]	my Numbers[5]	Exchange
5	**12**	**47**	**69**	**34**	25	39	69 > 34? Yes Swap and add to sorted sublist
6	**12**	**47**	**34**	69	25	39	check new sorted sublist. 47 > 34? Yes Swap
7	**12**	**34**	**47**	69	25	39	Check new sorted sublist 12 > 34? No No change in sorted sublist order. Note that the sorted sublist now contains three values

Comparison	my Numbers[0]	my Numbers[1]	my Numbers[2]	my Numbers[3]	my Numbers[4]	my Numbers[5]	Exchange
8	12	34	47	69	25	39	69 > 25? Yes Swap and add 25 to sorted sublist
9	12	34	47	25	69	39	check new sorted sublist. 47 > 25? Yes Swap
10	12	34	25	47	69	39	Check new sorted sublist 34 > 25? Yes Swap
11	12	25	34	47	69	39	Check new sorted sublist 12 > 25 ? No No change in sorted sublist Note that the sorted sublist now contains four values

Comparison	my Numbers[0]	my Numbers[1]	my Numbers[2]	my Numbers[3]	my Numbers[4]	my Numbers[5]	
12	12	25	34	47	69	39	69 > 39? Yes Swap and add 39 to sorted sublist
13	12	25	34	47	39	69	check new sorted sublist. 47 > 39? Yes Swap
14	12	25	34	39	47	69	Check new sorted sublist 34 > 39? No No Swap No further comparisons required in this pass.
	12	25	34	39	47	69	Data is now sorted

- The algorithms for both the bubble sort and the insertion sort are shown below using pseudo-code.

Bubble sort pseudo-code

```
For i= 0 to 4
        For j=0 to 4
                if myNumbers[j] > myNumbers
[j+1]
        SWAP NUMBERS
        end for
end for
SWAP NUMBERS
temp = myNumbers [j]
myNumbers [j] = myNumbers [j+1]
myNumbers [j+1] = temp
```

The bubble sort uses a loop (inside j loop) to move through an array comparing adjacent data items as it moves along. If an array element a[j] is greater than the element immediately to its right a[j+1], it swaps them. The first time around, this process will bubble the largest value to the end of the array. After N-1 passes the data will be sorted.

Insertion sort pseudo-code

```
For i= 0 to 5
        positionOfMin=i
        For j= i to 5
                If myNumbers[positionOfMin]
>myNumbers[j]
                        positionOfMin = j
        end for
    SWAP NUMBERS
end for
SWAP NUMBERS
Temp= myNumbers[i]
myNumbers[i]=myNumbers[positionOfMin]
myNumbers[positionOfMin] = temp
```

The insertion sort uses two loops. The first loop goes from 0 to 5, and the second loop goes from i to 5, so it goes from 0 to 5, then from 1 to 5, then from 2 to 5, etc.

This sort inserts each element of the array into its proper position, leaving larger stretches of the array sorted (the sorted sub-list); then, the current element of the array is inserted into the proper position at the head of the array.

Algorithms for searching

- Search algorithms are used to locate and return data given certain criteria. Each search algorithm has benefits and limitations.

The linear search algorithm

- Every data item is examined to see if it matches the target value.
- The average number of attempts required to find a target value is half the number of data items.
- It could take on average ten attempts to find a target value in a set of 20 data items.

Pseudo-code for a linear search through an array called myNumbers holding six data items

```
Declare array myNumbers
i=0
found = false
    For i= 0 to 5
        if myNumbers[i] = targetValue
            found=true
        endif
    end for
    If found = true
        OUTPUT MESSAGE "Target value found"
    Else
        OUTPUT MESSAGE "Target value not found"
```

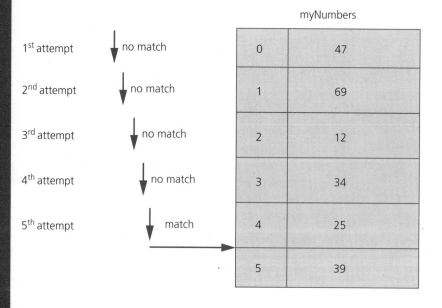

5 attempts in total to find 25.

The binary search algorithm

- The **binary search** algorithm is more efficient than the linear search algorithm.
- It only works on data that is already sorted.
- The binary search starts by finding the middle location in the list.
- The middle location value is compared to the target value. If the target value is not found, the search determines if the target value is below or above the middle location value.
- This process is repeated and the number of items being searched through the 'search space' is decreased until eventually there is only one item to be searched through.
- In a binary search, the maximum number of attempts required to find a target value is $\log_2$ number of items.

Binary search A search algorithm that works on a sorted list of data items – the target value is located by finding the mid-point location in the list and comparing that value to the target value – this is repeated until the target value is found or the search space has diminished to one item that is not the target value

- So, to find a target value in a set of 20 data items, the maximum number of attempts would be four. Compare this to the linear search.
- Consider the array myNumbers, which now contains 11 numbers sorted in numerical order.
- The target value = 85
- myNumbers

Location	0	1	2	3	4	5	6	7	8	9	10
Value	12	25	34	39	47	69	72	78	85	90	99

- To find 85:
  - Find the mid-point location, using start_location = 0 and end_location = 10.

```
mid = start_location + (end_location - start_
location)/2
mid = 0 + ((10-0)/2) = 5
```

Location	0	1	2	3	4	5	6	7	8	9	10
Value	12	25	34	39	47	69	72	78	85	90	99

```
Is the value in location 5 = to the target
value? No
Is the value in location 5 < target value? Yes
    Calculate a new start_location
        Start_location= mid + 1 = 5+1=6
        end_location remains the same = 10
```

  - The search space has been decreased. It is from location 6 to location 10 and includes only five data items.

Location	6	7	8	9	10
Value	72	78	85	90	99

  - Find the mid-point location using start_location = 6 and end_location = 10.
    mid = start_location + (end_location – start_location)/2
    mid = 6 + ((10-6)/2) = 8

Location	6	7	8	9	10
Value	72	78	85	90	99

- Is the value in location 8 = to the target value? Yes.
  - The target value has been found after two attempts. This is much more efficient than applying a linear search, which would have taken nine attempts.
- Pseudo-code for a binary search that uses an array of N numbers sorted in descending order and handles the situation when a number is not found might look like this:

```
Declare array myNumbers
start_location =0
end_location= N-1
found = false
while (start_location <= end_location)
mid = start_location +(end_location -start_location) / 2)
    if myNumbers[mid]=target
         found=true
    else
         if (target < myNumbers[mid])
             start_location = mid + 1;
             else
             if (target > myNumbers[mid])
                 end_location = mid - 1;
             end if
         end if
    end if
END While
If found = true
    OUTPUT MESSAGE "Target value found"
Else
    OUTPUT MESSAGE "Target value not found"
```

> **Common mistake**
> Ensure you calculate the mid-point accurately.

Refining a solution to a problem during design

REVISED

- The initial solution to a problem is unlikely to be perfect and will need some modification to ensure that it meets a set of requirements.
- The principles of computational thinking can help define a solution.
- An initial solution may omit aspects of functionality required by a user or may be inefficient.

> **Refining a solution** The process of reviewing the design for a solution and making necessary changes so that the design meets the user's requirements efficiently and accurately

Defining and refining a solution

- Consider the following problem: a student must create a program that will take as input a character representing a shape ('S' = square, 'C' = circle, 'T' = triangle), request the appropriate dimensions, calculate the area of the shape and output a suitable message to the user.

  (Assume the following formulas for area: circle = πr^2, square = length × breadth, triangle = ½ base × height.)

> **Common mistake**
> Always refer to the end user during refinement and design.

- Using decomposition, a list of sub-problems can be created as follows:
  - INPUT and validate shape
  - Request dimensions
  - OUTPUT area

  These are the main tasks required to solve the problem. They can be further divided up, meaning that the design can be further refined.

Now test yourself answers and glossary at www.hoddereducation.co.uk/myrevisionnotes

Refining and designing a solution

- The sub-problems can be further defined, to show each single step required to ensure the task is completed.

INPUT and validate shape	Request dimensions	OUTPUT area

do
 	
    valid=true
 	
    OUTPUT prompt
 	
    INPUT shape
 	
    if shape!='C' or shape!='S' or shape!='T'
 	
  valid=false
 	
  OUTPUT error message
 	
    end if
 	
    clear error message
 	
WHILE valid=false
	If shape='S'
	
	    OUTPUT prompt
	
	    INPUT length
	
	    INPUT breadth
	
	CALCULATE area = length * breadth
	
	else if shape = 'C'
	
	    OUTPUT prompt
	
	    INPUT radius
	
	CALCULATE area = 3.14 * radius * radius
	
	else if shape = 'T'
	
	    OUTPUT prompt
	
	    INPUT base
	
	    INPUT height
	
	CALCULATE area = 0.5 * base * height
	
	end if
		OUTPUT area

- Refinement is the process of reviewing the design for a solution and making necessary changes so that the design meets the user's requirements efficiently and accurately.
  - Refinements can be made to the design to ensure that the user will receive a product that meets their needs.
  - Possible refinements can be identified by examining the solution and by using a test plan to test the solution prior to writing the code.
  - The test plan will specify extreme, valid and invalid values to be input.
  - The test plan is used to test the functionality of the solution and the accuracy and appropriateness of the output to be produced from the solution.
  - Additional refinements can also come from the user if they are part of the design team.
- See also Chapter 12 for discussion of the role played by the end user when developing prototypes of a digital system.

Models for designing solutions

- The traditional development model is a model for creating a system that follows a sequential set of steps:
  - analysis, where the user's requirements are determined
  - design, where the solution is designed and refined
  - implementation, where the design is coded
  - testing, where the coded solution is tested using a variety of different methods
  - maintenance, where the system is changed or tweaked after it has been released to the user.
- An agile model is a method of developing a system where small sections are developed, tested and reviewed by the user. Feedback from the full development team, including the user, is used to improve the small section. Development happens in short bursts called 'sprints', which could last one to two weeks.

> **Data requirements** The data that a program or system uses, including data input, information output and any values to be stored temporarily during processing

Identifying data requirements for a solution

`REVISED`

- **Data requirements** are the data that a program or system uses, including data input, information output and any values to be stored temporarily during processing.
- Using the example above, this table shows some of the data requirements for the solution:

	Data item	Data type	Sample valid data	Function of data item
1	shape	character	C	Stores the character representing the type of shape
2	length	real/double/float	2.2	Stores length for a square shape
3	breadth	real/double/float	3.5	Stores breadth for a square shape
4	radius	real/double/float	1.75	Stores radius for a circle shape
5	base	real/double/float	3.0	Stores base for a triangle shape
6	height	real/double/float	4.0	Stores height for a triangle shape
7	area	real/double/float	12.45	Stores area for each shape; calculated using the relevant formula for each shape
8	valid	Boolean	true	Used to control the validation loop

- Data requirements are needed to produce a test plan for the system. The test plan is used to check that the program works as expected and is important for identifying errors in the logic of the design. These can be corrected and the design improved as a result.

Developing an appropriate user interface

`REVISED`

- The **user interface** is the part of the system the user interacts with.
- It should be:
  - easy to use, or 'user-friendly'
  - designed using colours, icons and messages in a consistent manner, placing menus, messages and buttons in the same place throughout the system
  - responsive and not have lengthy loading times

> **User interface** Any part of a system that the user can interact with; this includes data capture forms, menus and buttons

Now test yourself answers and glossary at www.hoddereducation.co.uk/myrevisionnotes

- o supportive of the user if they make a mistake, by providing helpful messages and feedback
  - o focused on user experience, have visual appeal and be attractive to the user.
- During design, the interface should be drawn using wireframes or sketches. This can be shown to the user, who can make suggestions about changes and the addition of features.
- Solutions can provide the user with a graphical user interface or a simple text-based screen that prompts the user for input.

Using a dry run to test a solution

REVISED

- A **dry run** is a paper-based exercise that allows the programmer to go through the solution on a step-by-step basis. The dry run highlights any errors in the logic of the solution.
- It can be used at the design or coding stages.
- It involves creating a trace table with a list of variables and checking the value of the variables after each line of code has been executed.
- This can identify errors in the logic of the design and any omissions and incorrect results.
- To create a trace table:
  - o Number each line of code or pseudo-code.
  - o Create a table structure.
  - o Create a column for each variable in the section of code.
  - o Add an output column to show any output generated from the code.
- Consider the section of pseudo-code used to validate the shape entered:

> **Dry run** A paper-based exercise that allows the programmer to go through the solution step by step; the dry run will highlight any errors in the logic of the solution

```
1  do
2      valid=true
3      OUTPUT prompt
4          INPUT shape
5              if shape!='C' or shape!='S' or shape!='T'
6      valid=false
7      OUTPUT error message
8      end if
9      clear error message
10     WHILE valid=false
```

Line no.	Valid	Shape	Output
1			
2	True		
3	True		Prompt
4	True	R	
5	True	R	
6	False	R	
7	False	R	Error message
8	False	R	
9	False	R	Cleared screen
10	False	R	

Line no.	Valid	Shape	Output
1	False		
2	True		
3	True		Prompt
4	True	C	
5	True	C	
9	True	C	Cleared screen
10	True	C	Loop ended

Exam tip

You should be able to understand a simple flowchart or pseudo-code, comment on its function and efficiency and create a trace table to test the solution.

Now test yourself

TESTED

1 Describe the main elements of computational thinking. [6 marks]
2 Consider the bubble sort and the insertion sort. Evaluate their efficiency in terms of the number of comparisons carried out within a sort and the number of exchanges carried out during a sort. [6 marks]
3 Explain two ways in which data can be searched. [4 marks]
4 A program is required that will take as input ten values representing the wages earned (in £) by ten employees. The wages should not exceed £200. The program should calculate and output the total and average wage for the group. Your output should be appropriately formatted.

 (a) Write an algorithm for the problem. [10 marks]
 (b) Create a trace table and conduct a dry run for the validation of the wages entered. [6 marks]
 (c) Recommend refinements following the dry-run exercise. [2 marks]

Revision activity

● Try writing a program to implement each sort and include a binary or linear search in your code. Remember there are a variety of solutions. Examine the efficiency of each sort and be able to comment on this.
● Ensure you can design an algorithm to solve problems. You should also be able to create a trace table using an algorithm and test a solution.
● Use your controlled assessment work to practise identifying data requirements for a solution.

22 Programming constructs

- Programs make use of a combination of features available in a programming language. Some of these key features are defined below.

Term	Definition	Example
Variable	A named location in computer memory used to hold data when a program is running: the value of a variable can change while the program is running. When declaring a variable it must be given a name and a data type.	Declare a variable called **number** to hold an integer value C#: int number Python: number=0 Note that variables do not need to be declared explicitly in Python in order to reserve memory space. The memory space is reserved as soon as the variable is assigned a value.
Constant	A named location in computer memory used to hold data when a program is running: the value of the constant remains the same while the program is running. When declaring a constant it must be given a name and a data type.	Declare a constant to hold a decimal value C#: Const float rateOfPay =11.55 Python: there is no constant keyword
Boolean operator	An operator that allows conditions to be combined and then evaluated: the outcome is a Boolean variable. These have been demonstrated in the previous chapter.	C#: the AND operator is denoted by &&. the OR operator is denoted by || Python: AND OR
Arithmetic operator	Enables arithmetic operations to be carried out on variables: arithmetic operators include +, −, * (multiply), /.	b*c
Input statement	A statement used to capture data which is to be used in the program.	C#: StudentName=Console.Readline() Python: StudentName=Input("Enter your name")
Output statement	A statement used to output data and information from the program	C#: Console.Write Python: print
Assignment statement	A statement that assigns a value to a variable, constant or other data structure: the value on the right-hand side of an assignment statement can contain a calculation.	a=b*c Assigns the value of b*c to the variable named a

> **Variable** A data value stored in memory that can change during program execution

- Examples of each of these features can be seen in the code samples within this chapter.

Program control structures

- Sequence: sequence denotes the order in which instructions are carried out by the computer. The simplest programs run from beginning to end and each statement is carried out one after the other in sequence.
- **Selection**: the sequence of instructions within a program can be changed based on the value of variables within that program. This means that certain statements are selected based on a value. This is achieved through the use of IF statements and Boolean operators.
- IF statement: when a condition in an IF statement evaluates to true, the statements following IF are executed. Otherwise, the statements following Else are executed. IF statements can be nested and conditions can be combined using Boolean operators to form complex selection statements.
- **Iteration**: iteration is another word for 'repetition'. Repetition is used when a section of code is to be carried out more than once. Programming languages facilitate repetition through loops. Repetition comes in two forms: unconditional and conditional.

> **Selection** Where only some lines of code need to be run and only if a certain condition is met; if the condition is not met, the code is not executed
>
> **Iteration** The use of loops and conditions to repeat sections of code

Exam tip

- Ensure that you understand the role of sequence, selection and iteration when creating a solution to a problem.
- Take time to construct conditions using Boolean operators and evaluate the conditions to true or false.

Unconditional or bounded repetition

- There is a start value and a stop value for the loop, for example when writing a program to output all the multiples of three between 3 and 99. This is unconditional repetition as the loop will repeat 97 times.
- The basic structure of a FOR loop is as follows:

```
FOR loopcontrolvariable = startvalue TO stopvalue
    section of code to be repeated
END For
```

- The loop control variable will be incremented by 1 each time the loop is executed. An increment of 1 is the default. It is possible to change the increment value within the FOR loop by adding additional code to the FOR statement.
- In C# the FOR loop is structured as follows: for(initialise;condition;increment).
  - Initialise: the loop control variable is initialised to the starting value once during the execution of the loop.
  - Condition: the condition is evaluated during each execution of the loop.
  - Increment: this part of the statement is used to update or change the loop control variable.

C#	Output

```csharp
1  using System;
2  using System.Collections.Generic;
3  using System.Linq;
4  using System.Text;
5  using System.Threading.Tasks;
6
7  namespace ConsoleApplication1
8  {
9      class Program
10     {
11         static void Main(string[] args)
12         {
13             for (int i = 3; i <= 99; i++)
14             {
15                 if (i % 3 == 0)
16                     Console.WriteLine(i + " is a multiple of 3");
17             }
18             Console.ReadKey();
19         }
20
21     }
22 }
```

```
3 is a multiple of 3
6 is a multiple of 3
9 is a multiple of 3
12 is a multiple of 3
15 is a multiple of 3
18 is a multiple of 3
21 is a multiple of 3
24 is a multiple of 3
27 is a multiple of 3
30 is a multiple of 3
33 is a multiple of 3
36 is a multiple of 3
```

Python	

```python
for number in range(3,99):  #to iterate between 3 to 99
# use the modulus function which returns the remainder after division
    if number%3 == 0:
        print (str(number) + " is a multiple of 3")
```

```
3 is a multiple of 3
6 is a multiple of 3
9 is a multiple of 3
12 is a multiple of 3
15 is a multiple of 3
18 is a multiple of 3
21 is a multiple of 3
24 is a multiple of 3
27 is a multiple of 3
30 is a multiple of 3
33 is a multiple of 3
36 is a multiple of 3
```

Conditional or unbounded repetition

● The loop will run until a particular condition is true or false. Consider
writing a program that ensures that a user enters an integer value
between 1 and 50. A Boolean variable can be used to control the loop.
Using a Boolean variable called 'valid', the algorithm could be:

```
number=0
valid=False
While (valid is False)
    OUTPUT "Enter a number in the range 1 - 50"
    If (number >=1 AND number <=50)
        valid=True
    Else
        OUTPUT Error Message
    END-IF
END WHILE
```

- Programming languages also provide a loop that tests the condition at the end of the loop.

```
number=0
valid=False
do
    OUTPUT "Enter a number in the range 1 - 5"
    If (number >=1 AND number <=50)
        valid=True
    Else
        OUTPUT Error Message
    END-IF
While (valid is False)
```

- When a loop has the condition at the beginning, the code within the loop may not be executed at all if the condition evaluates to false.
- When a loop has the condition at the end, the code within the loop is executed at least once because the condition is not tested until after the code is executed.

One-dimensional arrays

REVISED

- An array is a data structure that holds a set of data items of the same data type. The array is assigned a name, a size (representing the number of data items to be stored) and a data type by the programmer.
- An array of integers called myNumbers has been used in the sorting algorithms in the previous chapter. The array has six integer values stored: 47, 69, 12, 34, 25, 39. An individual data item or element is accessed by referring to the array name and the index of the element.

Element	my Numbers[0]	my Numbers[1]	my Numbers[2]	my Numbers[3]	my Numbers[4]	my Numbers[5]
Position in array [index]	0	1	2	3	4	5
Value	47	69	12	34	25	39

- Key facts about arrays:
  - The computer reserves a set of memory locations, one for each element in the array. The memory locations are next to each other, or 'contiguous'.
  - In many programming languages, arrays are zero-indexed. This means that the index of the first element in the array is 0. So, myNumbers[0] holds a value of 47.
  - Elements can be assigned values, for example myNumbers[2]=99.

Exam tip

Practise using loops to process elements within an array.

- An array is described using a declaration statement, for example declaring an array called myNumbers that will hold six integers: C# int[ ] myNumbers = new int[6].
- Python uses lists and tuples instead of arrays. Tuples can hold mixed data types.
- To access every element in the array, a loop can be used.
- You can see examples of the use of sequence, iteration, selection and **one-dimensional arrays** in the code sections following.

Programming sort algorithms

REVISED

Programming the bubble sort

- The **bubble sort** is a simple sort that compares adjacent elements. Below is one implementation of the bubble sort.
  - C#:

> **Bubble sort** A simple sort method that repeatedly steps through a list of data items; adjacent elements are compared and swapped if they are in the wrong order

ConsoleApplication1.Program

```csharp
1  using System;
2  using System.Collections.Generic;
3  using System.Linq;
4  using System.Text;
5  using System.Threading.Tasks;
6
7  namespace ConsoleApplication1
8  {
9      class Program
10     {
11         static void Main(string[] args)
12         {
13             int[]  mynumbers = {47, 69, 12, 34, 25, 39};
14             int temp;
15             for (int i=0;i<mynumbers.Length-1;i++)
16             {
17                 for (int j=0;j<mynumbers.Length-1-i;j++)
18                     if (mynumbers[j] > mynumbers[j + 1])
19                     {
20                         temp = mynumbers[j];
21                         mynumbers[j] = mynumbers[j + 1];
22                         mynumbers[j + 1] = temp;
23                     }
24                 Console.WriteLine("After pass {0}", i + 1);
25                 for (int k = 0; k < mynumbers.Length; k++)
26                     Console.Write(mynumbers[k] +" ");
27                 Console.WriteLine();
28
29             }
30             Console.WriteLine("Sorted List");
31             for (int i = 0; i < mynumbers.Length; i++)
32                 Console.Write(mynumbers[i]+ " ");
33             Console.WriteLine();
34             Console.ReadKey();
35
36         }
37     }
38 }
```

○ Python:

```python
mynumbers = [47, 69, 12, 34, 25, 39]
for index in range(1,len(mynumbers)):

    currentvalue = mynumbers[index]
    position = index

    while position>0 and mynumbers[position-1]>currentvalue:
        mynumbers[position]=mynumbers[position-1]
        position = position-1


    mynumbers[position]=currentvalue
    print ("After pass " + str(index)+ " "),
    print(mynumbers)

print("The sorted list is : "),
print(mynumbers)
```

Programming the insertion sort

● Below is one implementation of this **sort**.

```csharp
9    class Program
10   {
11       static void Main(string[] args)
12       {
13
14           //declare an array which will hold a set of integer values
15           int[] mynumbers = {47, 69, 12, 34, 25, 39};
16           //declare the variables to be used in the sorting code
17           int currentvalue, position, index;
18
19           //for loop to go from first number to last number
20           for (index=0;index<mynumbers.Length; index++)
21           {
22               currentvalue = mynumbers[index];
23               position = index;
24               //while loop to find where to insert the value in the sublist
25               while ((position>0) && (mynumbers[position-1]>currentvalue))
26               {
27               mynumbers[position]=mynumbers[position-1];
28               position = position-1;
29               }
30
31               mynumbers[position]=currentvalue;
32               Console.WriteLine ("After pass {0} ", index+1);
33               for (int i=0;i<mynumbers.Length;i++)
34                   Console.Write(mynumbers[i] + " ");
35               Console.WriteLine();
36           }
37
38           Console.WriteLine("The sorted list is: ");
39           //note that the code below is repeated from above
40           //this is not good coding practice.  In this case the code should be
41           //written as a function and called when required.  This will be addressed
42           // later in the chapter.
43               for (int i=0;i<mynumbers.Length;i++)
44                   Console.Write(mynumbers[i] + " ");
45           Console.WriteLine();
46           Console.ReadKey();
47
48       }
```

> **Insertion sort** A simple sorting algorithm that builds a sorted sub-list one item at a time; the sub-list becomes the new sorted list

Programming the linear search

- A **linear search** is not efficient as it compares all elements in the array during a search. Below is the code for the algorithms discussed in the previous chapter.
  - C#:

> **Linear search** A simple search algorithm that compares every data item in a list to the target value

```
ConsoleApplication1.Program                                          ▾  Main(string[] args)
 1  using System;
 2  using System.Collections.Generic;
 3  using System.Linq;
 4  using System.Text;
 5  using System.Threading.Tasks;
 6
 7  namespace ConsoleApplication1
 8  {
 9      class Program
10      {
11          static void Main(string[] args)
12          {
13              int[] mynumbers = new int[20];
14              Boolean found = false;
15
16              Console.WriteLine("Enter the twenty numbers to be stored in the array");
17              for (int i = 0; i < 20; i++)
18              {
19                  mynumbers[i] = Convert.ToInt32(Console.ReadLine());
20              }
21
22              Console.WriteLine("Enter a number that you wish to search for\n");
23              int searchNumber = Convert.ToInt32(Console.ReadLine());
24              for (int i = 0; i<20; i++)
25              {
26                  if (mynumbers[i] == searchNumber)
27                  {
28                      Console.Write("Number {0} found ", searchNumber );
29                      Console.WriteLine("at location {0}\n",i + 1);
30                      found = true;
31                  }
32              }
33
34              if (found==false)
35                  Console.WriteLine("Number not found");
36              Console.ReadKey();
37
38          }
39      }
40  }
```

  - Python:

```
mynumbers=[47,69,12,34,25,39]
foundmatch=False
searchnum=int(input("Enter number to search for "))
for i in range(1,len(mynumbers)):
    if (mynumbers[i]==searchnum):
            foundmatch=True
            print("Number found at position ", i)
if(foundmatch==False):
    print ("number not found")
```

Programming the binary search

- The algorithm for the **binary search** is discussed in the previous chapter. Below is an implementation of the binary search using a sorted one-dimensional array of integers.

> **Binary search** A search algorithm that works on a sorted list of data items; the target value is located by finding the mid location in the list and comparing that value to the target value – this is repeated until the target value is found or the search space has diminished to one item that is not the target value

```
10        {
11  ⊟        static void Main(string[] args)
12            {
13
14                int[] mynumbers = { 6, 5, 4, 3, 2, 1 };
15                Boolean found = false;
16                int mid=0, first = 0, last = mynumbers.Length - 1;
17                Console.WriteLine("What number are you looking for");
18                string item = Console.ReadLine();
19                int target = Convert.ToInt16(item);
20
21                //for a sorted array with descending values
22                while( (first <= last) && (found==false))
23                {
24                    mid = first + (last-first) / 2;
25                    if ( mynumbers[mid]==target)
26                        found=true;
27                    else
28                    if (target < mynumbers[mid])
29                        first = mid + 1;
30                    else
31                    if (target > mynumbers[mid])
32                        last = mid - 1;
33                }
34
35                if (found == true)
36                    Console.WriteLine("Value found at position " + mid);
37                else
38                    Console.WriteLine("Value not found");
39                Console.ReadKey();
40            }
41        }
42  }
```

String manipulation

- Data containing text, letters or a mixture of letters and numbers are known as strings. Strings can be processed and manipulated using string functions.
- Consider two strings:
  - string1="WELL DONE"
  - string2="award-winning performance"
- Each character in the string has a position and a value. Strings are zero-indexed.

Position	0	1	2	3	4	5	6	7	8
	string1[0]	string1[1]	string1[2]	string1[3]	string1[4]	string1[5]	string1[6]	string1[7]	string1[8]
Value	W	E	L	L		D	O	N	E

● There are many string handling functions available. Some of the more common functions are listed below.

String handling function	C#	Python
Splitting a string	string1.split(" ") Split string one at the first space Result: "WELL"	String1.split('') Split string one at the first space Result: ['WELL', 'DONE']
Concatenating string: appending strings together using the relevant function or symbol	string1 + " " + string2 Concatenate string1, a space and string 2 Result: "WELL DONE award-winning performance"	string1 + " " + string2 Concatenate string1, a space and string 2 Result: "WELL DONE award-winning performance"
Character and substring searching: in a string for the occurrence of a character or substring. This search returns an integer representing the starting position of the substring or position of the character in the string being searched.	string1.IndexOf("D") find the position of the first letter "D" in string1 Result: 5	string1.index('D') find the position of the first letter "D" in string1 Result: 5
Substring searching: using a start position and a length, return a substring.	string2.Substring(6, 7) Start at position 6 in string2 and return the next 7 characters result: "winning"	string2[6:13] Start at position 6 in string2 and return the next 7 characters result: "winning"
Lower case: change all the characters in a string to lower case.	string1.ToLower(); Change all letters in string1 to lowercase Result: "well done"	string1.lower() Change all letters in string1 to lowercase Result: "well done"
Upper case: change all the characters in a string to upper case.	string2.ToUpper(); Change all letters in string2 to uppercase Result: "AWARD-WINNING PERFORMANCE"	string2.upper() Change all letters in string2 to uppercase Result: "AWARD-WINNING PERFORMANCE"
Length: return an integer value representing the length of a string.	string2.Length(); Return the length of string2 Result: 25	len(string2) Return the length of string2 Result: 25

C#

```
12          {
13              string string1 = "WELL DONE";
14              string string2 = "award winning performance";
15
16              //finding the length of a string
17              Console.WriteLine("String 1 has {0} characters\n", string1.Length);
18              Console.WriteLine("String 2 has {0} characters\n", string2.Length);
19
20
21              //split a string up into smaller strings
22              //this statement splits string1 each time a space is found and puts the resulting
23              //string into an array of type string
24              string[] thewords = string1.Split(' ');
25
26              Console.WriteLine("Splitting string 1 into words gives:");
27
28              foreach (string s in thewords) //using the foreach loop to print the contents of thewords
29                  Console.WriteLine(s);
30
31              //concatenating two strings places the strings together as one string
32              string fullstring = string1 + " " + string2;
33
34              //search for the occurence of a word or character
35              int wordposition = fullstring.IndexOf("winning");
36              Console.WriteLine("The word winning has been found at position {0} in this string", wordposition);
37
38              //copy string1 to a new string called copystring1
39              string copystring1 = string.Copy(string1);
40              Console.WriteLine("copystring1= "+ copystring1);
41
42              //replace the word "done" in string 1 with "completed"
43              string newstring1 = copystring1.Replace("DONE", "completed");
44              Console.WriteLine("newstring1= " + newstring1);
45
46              //copy 7 letters from string2 starting at position 6 in the string and place them into mysubstring
47              string mysubstring = string2.Substring(6, 7);
48              Console.WriteLine("mysubstring = "+ mysubstring);
49
50              string1 = string1.ToLower();
51              Console.WriteLine("Lower case string1= "+ string1);
52              string2 = string2.ToUpper();
53              Console.WriteLine("Upper case string2= " + string2);
54              Console.ReadKey();
55          }
56      }
```

Output

```
String 1 has 9 characters

String 2 has 25 characters

Splitting string 1 into words gives:
WELL
DONE
The word winning has been found at position 16 in this string
copystring1= WELL DONE
newstring1= WELL completed
mysubstring= winning
Lower case string1= well done
Upper case string2= AWARD WINNING PERFORMANCE
```

Python

```python
string1 = 'WELL DONE'
string2 = 'award winning performance'

#finding the length of a string
print("String 1 has ", len(string1), "characters")
print("String 2 has ", len(string2), "characters")


#split a string up into smaller strings
#this statement splits string1 each time a space is found and puts the resulting
#string into an array of type string
thewords = string1.split(' ')

print("Splitting string 1 into words gives:");
print (thewords)

#concatenating two strings places the strings together as one string
fullstring = string1+" "+ string2
#search for the occurence of a word or character
wordposition = fullstring.index("winning")
print("The word winning has been found at position ", wordposition, " in this string")

#copy string1 to a new string called copystring1
copystring1 = string1
print("copystring1= "+ copystring1)

#replace the word "done" in string 1 with "completed"
newstring1 = copystring1.replace("DONE", "completed");
print("newstring1= " + newstring1);

#copy 7 letters from string2 starting at position 6 in the string and place them into mysubstring
#string mysubstring = string2.Substring(6, 7);
#Console.WriteLine("mysubstring = "+ mysubstring);

string1 = string1.lower()
string2 = string2.upper()
print ("Lower case string1 = ", string1)
print ("Upper case string2 = ", string2)
```

```
String 1 has  9 characters
String 2 has  25 characters
Splitting string 1 into words gives:
['WELL', 'DONE']
The word winning has been found at position  16  in this string
copystring1= WELL DONE
newstring1= WELL completed
Lower case string1 =  well done
Upper case string2 =  AWARD WINNING PERFORMANCE
>>>
```

Building reusable code

REVISED

- If a section of code is to be used in more than one place, a function or method can be written. Functions or methods are blocks of code that can be reused within a program.
- They are written to perform a particular task and can be 'called' when required within the program.

- Key facts about functions (or methods):
  - o Functions are given a name.
  - o Data in the form of parameters can be passed to functions.
  - o Functions can also return data.
  - o Functions give programmers the opportunity to structure code so that it is more efficient.
  - o Functions can be reused within a program.

Basic file handling

REVISED

- Files provide a means of permanently storing data. When a program uses data, it is lost after the program stops running. Files allow data to be stored permanently after the program closes. The data in the file can be used as input to the program also.

```
11      class Program
12      {
13          static void ReadData()
14          {
15              FileStream myFile = new FileStream("test.txt", FileMode.Open, FileAccess.Read);
16              StreamReader myStream = new StreamReader(myFile);
17              Console.WriteLine("Program to show content of test file");
18              myStream.BaseStream.Seek(0, SeekOrigin.Begin);
19              string str = myStream.ReadLine();
20
21              while (str != null)
22              {
23                  Console.WriteLine(str);
24                  str = myStream.ReadLine();
25              }
26
27              Console.ReadKey();
28              myStream.Close();
29              myFile.Close();
30
31          }
32
33          static void WriteData()
34          {
35              //create a filestream
36              FileStream myFile = new FileStream("test.txt", FileMode.Append, FileAccess.Write);
37              StreamWriter myStream = new StreamWriter(myFile);
38              Console.WriteLine("Enter the text which you want to write to the file");
39              string str = Console.ReadLine();
40              myStream.WriteLine(str);
41              myStream.Flush();
42              myStream.Close();
43              myFile.Close();
44          }
45
46          static void Main(string[] args)
47
48          {
49              WriteData();
50              ReadData();
51          }
52
53      }
54
55  }
```

Sample C# program showing simple file-handling operations

```
#Open a text file
myFile = open("myFile.txt", "r")

#reading from a text file:
myFile = open("myFile.txt","r")
print (myFile.read())

#reading lines from the file
myFile = open("myFile.txt", "r")
print (myFile.readline())

#reading a set of lines from the file
myFile = open("myFile.txt.", "r")
print (myFile.readlines())

f = open("myFile.txt")
next = f.read(1)
while next != "":
    print(next)
    next = f.read(1)

#writing to a file
myFile = open("myFile.txt","w")
myFile.write("This is a test\n")
myFile.close()

#writing multiple lines of text to a file
myFile = open("myFile.txt", "w")
lines_of_text = ["This is the second test", "This is the third test", "This is the fourth test"]
myFile.writelines(lines_of_text)
myFile.close()

#appending data to the file
myFile = open("myFile.txt", "a")
myFile.write("A fourth test")
myFile.close


#closing a file
myFile = open("myFile.txt", "r")
print(myFile.read())
myFile.close()
```

Sample Python program showing simple file-handling operations

Now test yourself

TESTED ☐

1 (a) Explain the following key terms: variable, constant and Boolean operator. [6 marks]

(b) Write an algorithm that represents a solution to the following problem:
Take as input a number representing a student's percentage mark in an examination and ensure the percentage is a valid value. [5 marks]

(c) Write a program that will take as input ten values representing students' percentages in an examination. The program should sort the values and output the contents of the sorted array. [6 marks]

2 Describe two methods of searching and explain which method is more efficient and why. [6 marks]

3 (a) How do functions (or methods) help improve the quality of code? [3 marks]

(b) Using the problem outlined in part 1(c), reorganise the program to include a function called outputData, which will output the contents of the sorted array. [6 marks]

(c) Why is file handling an important feature of programming languages? [3 marks]

Revision activity

● Review the bubble sort and the insertion sort and identify the programming constructs used in each case.
● Reflect on the use of functions or methods and provide an explanation of how they can make the code more efficient.
● Learn the definitions for key words such as variable, constant and Boolean operator.

23 Simple error-handling techniques

Data validation

- **Data validation** is necessary to ensure that data entered is complete, falls within a set of boundaries specified within the code and is sensible. It aims to reduce the amount of erroneous data captured by the program or system.
- Data validation can be performed using presence, range, type, length and format checks.

Validation check	Example of use
A **presence check** is used to ensure that the user has not left a value or field blank.	In forms to ensure that all fields are completed
A **range check** is used to ensure that the data entered is in the correct range. Range checks make use of upper and lower boundaries.	Used to ensure when entering a percentage that the value is in the range 0–100
A **length check** is used to ensure that the entered data does not exceed or is not shorter than a particular number of characters.	Used to ensure that a password has a minimum number of characters
A **type check** is used to ensure that the data entered is of the correct data type.	Used to ensure that a numeric value is entered when completing calculations
A **format check** is used to ensure that data entered is in the correct format. This means that the data must conform to a pattern.	Used to ensure that a postcode must have the following pattern: XX99 9XX, e.g. BT67 8LH

> **Data validation** Carried out by a computer automatically when data is input; it ensures that data is reasonable, sensible and within acceptable limits
>
> **Presence check** Used to ensure that the user has entered data and has not left a value or field blank; this is commonly used in forms to ensure that all fields are completed
>
> **Length check** Used to ensure that the user has entered data that does not exceed or is not shorter than a particular number of characters; this type of check is commonly used when entering a password to ensure that it contains a minimum amount of characters
>
> **Type check** Used to ensure that the data entered is of the correct data type, e.g. numeric, string, date
>
> **Format check** Used to ensure that data entered is in the correct format; this means that the data must conform to a pattern, e.g. a postcode must have the pattern XX99 9XX, where X is a letter 'A' to 'Z' and 9 is a digit '0' to '9'

> **Exam tip**
>
> You should be able to describe each validation check, give suitable examples to illustrate your answer and select the correct data validation method for a given situation.

Detection and correction techniques

- **Syntax errors** occur when the program is being entered into the editor and are detected when the program is being compiled. A program with syntax errors will not compile.
- Execution errors, or run-time errors, are detected during program execution and will cause the program to crash. Division by zero will cause a runtime error.
- Logic errors arise in programs that compile and run without error. The output produced by the program does not match the expected output. These errors are detected during testing.

> **Syntax error** An error in the code entered into the code editor, e.g. a misspelling or the omission of a symbol

Simple error-trapping techniques

REVISED

- Debugging is the process of detecting and correcting or removing errors from the code. It may involve using the debug feature of the programming language, creating breakpoints and stepping through code one line at a time.
- Exception or error handling is the process where a program will attempt to deal with an error generated at run time so that the program does not crash. When the error occurs, an exception is raised that 'calls' code to handle the error. An unhandled exception will still cause the program to crash. Programmers can make use of in-built exception-handling features and write customised code to handle specific errors.

Now test yourself

TESTED

1 What is the purpose of data validation? [2 marks]
2 Describe the different validation checks available and give examples of where each one can be used. [10 marks]
3 Describe the difference between syntax and execution errors. [3 marks]
4 Describe how errors can be trapped and corrected using a typical integrated development environment. [6 marks]

Revision activity

- Using a program that you have already written, investigate a debug facility.
- Describe how the debug feature enables the correction of errors.
- Generate syntax, execution and logic errors and record how the IDE (integrated development environment) deals with these errors.

Now test yourself answers and glossary at www.hoddereducation.co.uk/myrevisionnotes

24 Developing test plans and testing a solution

- Testing is also discussed in Chapter 7.
- The overall aim of testing is to improve the quality of the software by ensuring that it is bug-free, meets the user requirements and operates efficiently. This is done by testing the system. Errors or bugs are identified and subsequently fixed.
- Testing is a continuous process that is carried out throughout the development process.
- Testing needs to be planned, designed, executed and recorded. Developers build a number of **test cases**, which represent a wide variety of possible inputs to the program.

> **Test case** A document that contains a set of tests to help the programmer verify that the code works as expected. It will include expected results and actual outcomes

White box testing

REVISED

- **White box testing** tests the internal logic of a section of code to identify errors in syntax, logic and data flow.
- The tester needs to know how the code works, so a programmer completes this testing.
- White box tests are carried out on units of code.
- Test cases should be built so that every statement is executed at least once.

> **White box testing** A method of testing which examines the underlying structure of the application or code which has been developed

Advantages of white box testing	Disadvantages of white box testing
• Thorough, because it allows each line of code to be tested • Hidden errors are identified and the code is modified and optimised • Programmers who know the code can easily identify suitable test data	• Experienced programmers are required to undertake the testing • Large-scale applications require complex test cases, which is time-consuming • Some conditions may not be tested as it is not possible to test every possibility

> **Exam tip**
>
> You should be able to describe both black box testing and white box testing.

Black box testing

REVISED

- **Black box testing** focuses on testing inputs and outputs.
- It is used to identify errors in data structures, problems with user interfaces, errors in reports, missing functionality and behaviour errors.
- The tester has no knowledge of the internal code, so a variety of personnel carry out this type of testing.
- The unit of code is viewed as a black box (the tester cannot see inside the box).

> **Black box testing** Where the tester is unaware of the internal structure of the application they are testing

Advantages of black box testing	Disadvantages of black box testing
• Can help identify where the user requirements are not being met • Testers do not need to know about the code and so the tester can be independent of the developer • Test cases can be designed as soon as the specification for the unit is completed	• Not all program pathways are tested as only a small number of input cases are used • The reason for a test failure cannot be determined • Repetition of tests already carried out by the programmer may occur

Unit, integration and system testing

REVISED

Unit testing

- A unit of code is tested to ensure that it works as expected.
- The **unit test** has no relationship to code outside of the unit being tested.
- Unit testing starts with the module specification and includes detailed testing of the code.
- It is a form of white box testing with a narrow scope limited to one unit.

Unit testing Testing one module or unit of code to ensure that it is working as expected. The logic of the code is tested

Exam tip

You need to know how unit, integration and system testing is used when developing software.

Integration testing

- **Integration testing** occurs after unit testing.
- A number of tested units are combined together to form a sub-system.
- Integration testing is used to ensure that units are working together as expected, for example there will be a focus on the data passed between units.
- Integration tests identify problems with interfaces or with the interactions between units.

Integration testing When a number of units have been tested they are combined together to form a sub-system. Integration testing ensures that all of the units work together correctly

System testing

- **System testing** is carried out after integration testing.
- Sub-systems are brought together to form a complete software system. The system is tested as a whole to ensure that it meets the user requirements.
- The system is treated like a black box.
- This testing can help identify missing functionality or issues related to performance.
- The tests should be carried in a real-life setting with real volumes of data.

System testing Carried out on a complete and fully integrated system to ensure correct outputs are produced in compliance with the user requirements document

Creating and using a test plan

REVISED

- A test plan is a document that describes in detail the activities to be undertaken when testing is carried out.
- The list below details the expected contents of a test plan.

Now test yourself answers and glossary at www.hoddereducation.co.uk/myrevisionnotes

Introduction: a summary of the application or particular area of the application to be tested.

Features to be tested/not tested: any area not being tested should be identified with an explanation as to why it is not being tested, for example an existing application unaffected by new developments may not need to be tested at this point.

Testing approach (white box, black box. integration, system, unit).

Test environment (the hardware and software platform being used to support testing).

Staff involvement (details of any staff involved in the testing process).

Test schedule (details of any key dates in the testing schedule, for example a timeline detailing start and completion dates for different types of tests to be carried out).

Test strategy: this should include:

- ▲ a number for each individual test so that each test can be identified separately in the testing evidence
- ▲ a description of the area to be tested, for example whether it is a particular query or a navigational element of the application
- ▲ examples of the test data to be applied to the particular area of the application
- ▲ expected outcomes from the completed test
- ▲ actual test outcomes
- ▲ comments about the outcome of the test or details of any corrections made to the application.

- Testing during development is largely carried out by the development team and involves white box and black box testing. It should always be cross-referenced to the user requirements and seek to determine to what extent the user requirements were met.
- Testing should confirm that the software:
  - ○ meets the user requirements, both functional and non-functional
  - ○ operates efficiently and effectively.
- Non-functional requirements may include performance or response times for the processing of data and particular requirements in terms of usability.

Devising and using valid, invalid and extreme test data

REVISED

- Test cases, in the form of test data, must be created in order to test the system.
- The behaviour of the system is observed, recorded and compared to the expected outcome in the test plan.
- Test cases should include extreme data, valid data, invalid data and null data.

> **Extreme data** Used to test that the system can cope with very large or very small data values
>
> **Valid data** Used to test that the system operates as expected with normal data

- **Extreme data** is used to test that the system can cope with very large or very small data values, for example if a student number has to be in the range 1–100, the test data would normally include the numbers 1 and 100 as extreme values.
- **Valid data** is used to test that the system operates as expected with normal data.
- **Invalid data** is used to test that the system can process invalid data and does not crash when invalid data is entered.
- **Null data** is used to test that the system can cope when no data is entered.
- A simple test plan for the code that validates the student number in the range 1– 100 is shown below.

Invalid data Used to test that the system can process invalid data and does not crash when invalid data is entered

Null data Used to test that the system can cope when no data is entered

Common mistake

During test plan creation, ensure you do not omit important test data, e.g. null data.

Test number	Reason for test	Test data	Expected output	Observed output	Does observed match expected? (Y/N)
1	Extreme value	1	Value accepted		
2	Extreme value	100	Value accepted		
3	Invalid data	–23	Error message		
4	Valid data	25	Value accepted		
5	NULL test	No data – press Enter	Error message		

Now test yourself

TESTED ☐

1 What is the purpose of testing? [2 marks]
2 Describe both black box and white box testing and state the advantages and disadvantages of each. [8 marks]
3 (a) Describe the following methods of testing: unit, system and integration testing. [6 marks]
   (b) How can these types of testing help identify errors or problems with software? [3 marks]
4 (a) List the content of a test plan. [4 marks]
   (b) Describe how valid, invalid, null and extreme data can be used in testing. Give one example of how you have used each one. [6 marks]

Exam tip

Ensure you can create and complete a test plan that incorporates valid, invalid, extreme and null data for given scenarios.

Revision activity

- Using a program that you have already written, create a test plan that incorporates valid, invalid, null and extreme data.

25 Evaluation of digitally authored systems

- See Chapter 18 sections 'Evaluation', 'Evidencing an evaluation' and 'Points to consider', in conjunction with this chapter.
- Evaluating a system involves testing and reviewing the system to ensure that it meets the **user requirements** and is a full, **robust** and efficient solution.
  - An efficient solution includes code written in small reusable sections that has an acceptable response time when operated by the user.
- Evaluation is a continuous activity that should be carried out through the development of a system.
- Evaluation may lead to change and improvement of the product being developed.
- An evaluation can be undertaken throughout the design process, when the product has been developed, when handing the product over to the user or by the development team at the close of a project.
- An evaluation takes account of the outcome from user acceptance testing, when the product is tested using real data provided by the user.
- The result of an evaluation is written in a structured document (see Chapter 18 section 'Evidencing an evaluation').
- A range of personnel should be involved in the evaluation process, including members of the development team, the client company and the end user.
- An evaluation report should be structured and include details about the purpose of the evaluation, the timing and stage of development of the evaluation, the outcome of any previous evaluations of the product, and the names and roles of those involved.
- An evaluation should contain evidence to support any statements made about the quality of the system.
- Sources of evidence include the outcome from testing, documented interviews and observations.
- The development team may undertake an evaluation that includes looking at their own performance, team contribution, management of budget, time management and user feedback.
- Areas for improvement will be used as learning points for future projects.

> **User requirements**
> A document that details what the end user expects the system to do; it often forms part of a contract between the developer and the end user
>
> **Robustness** A measure of the system's ability to continue to run when high volumes of valid, exceptional or invalid data are entered

> **Exam tip**
> - Ensure you understand the importance of an evaluation in improving the quality of your system.
> - Learn the different ways in which evaluation of a system can take place, e.g. by using a test plan cross-referenced to the user requirements or by using test data supplied by programmers.
> - Learn the purpose of evaluation and how it is recorded.

Functional and non-functional user requirements

REVISED

- The user requirements can be described as a set of tasks that the software should perform in order to solve the problem described by the user.
- The list is created as a result of a detailed consultation between the user and the development team.
- The user requirements form the basis for evaluating the software developed.

- A test plan cross-referenced to the user requirements can determine the extent to which the proposed system will meet the user requirements.
- User requirements can be divided into functional and non-functional:
  - Functional requirements describe the things that the system should be able to do, for example produce a total value or output a particular report. These can be easily identified by examining the user requirements.
  - Non-functional requirements describe the way in which the system should work, for example the performance of the system in terms of user response time, the usability of the system and the reliability of the system.

Robustness

- The ability of a system to handle valid, invalid and exceptional data is a measure of its robustness.
- If the system does not crash when processing high volumes of valid, invalid or exceptional data, then we can say it is robust.
- A good test plan can help predict the robustness of the system

Common mistake

Do not think that evaluation occurs only after a software product has been fully developed – remember that it can occur throughout development.

Now test yourself

TESTED

1 Explain the term 'user requirements'. [3 marks]
2 Describe the purpose of evaluation (refer to Chapter 18). [4 marks]
3 List the contents of an evaluation report (refer to Chapter 18). [4 marks]
4 Describe the points that need to be considered when undertaking an evaluation (refer to Chapter 18). [4 marks]
5 How can a test plan help in the evaluation process? [4 marks]
6 What is 'robustness' when used to describe software and how can it be evaluated? [3 marks]

Revision activity

- Carry out an evaluation on a program that you or someone else has written. Report on the result of the evaluation by commenting on the extent to which the program meets the user requirements and its robustness.
- Make a list of suggested improvements and give a reason for each one.

Examination guidance

The CCEA Digital Technology GCSE is available in two pathways: Multimedia or Programming.

Assessment	Weighting	Units	
External written exam 1 hour	30%	Compulsory core unit: Unit 1 Digital Technology	
		Multimedia pathway	**Programming pathway**
External written exam 1 hour 30 minutes	40%	Unit 2 Digital Authoring Concepts	Unit 4 Digital Development Concepts
Controlled assessment A total of 36 hours are available for completion of the controlled assessment task. The total mark for the controlled assessment task is 60.	30%	Unit 3 Digital Authoring Practice	Unit 5 Digital Development Practice

You will therefore take two examinations: Unit 1 and either Unit 2 or Unit 4.

In your answers, you should show knowledge and understanding as stated in the assessment objectives for the unit. The specification can be downloaded from www.ccea.org.uk

Some questions on the examination paper will assess the quality of written communication (QWC). These responses are not only assessed on how many correct points are made, but also levelled in relation to correct use of technical terminology, spelling, punctuation and grammar. The QWC questions will be identified on the cover page of the examination paper.

Students are expected to take at least 40 per cent of the assessment at the end of the course, which means that the Unit 2 or Unit 4 examination must be taken at the end of the GCSE taught course.

The examination paper

Each examination paper will consist of compulsory structured questions; this means that you must answer all the questions. None of the questions will be worth more than 6 marks.

The types of question will include:
- Multiple-choice questions
- Cloze questions where you complete sentences using a range of words provided
- True or false questions
- Matching technical terms with their definitions
- Questions requiring an extended written response.

In the Unit 1 paper, you may be asked to:
- Expand acronyms
- Use real-life examples of digital technology in your answers.

In the Unit 2 paper, you may be asked to apply your design/practical skills to provide solutions to given problems.

In the Unit 4 paper, you may be asked:

- Structured questions that require you to apply your skills to develop solutions, for example by using algorithms, pseudo-code and flowcharts
- Detailed description questions that require you to evaluate approaches to problem solving
- Calculation questions using binary, denary and hexadecimal number bases
- Problem-based questions that require you to create, evaluate and/or test a solution to a given problem.

The stem of the question will contain a key word indicating how it should be answered, for example:

- Describe: give details about the technology, application or process
- Discuss: explain a concept and give an example to illustrate it; refer to its advantages and disadvantages
- Explain: give a reason why, for example a reason why a particular technology is the most appropriate for a given scenario
- List: provide a specific number of items
- State: briefly outline any points relevant to the context referred to in the question
- Evaluate: make a judgement regarding the technology or application in the question. Refer to the main features of the application or technology, and consider its pros and cons.

Preparing for the examination

- Use a small notebook to create a list for each topic of all the acronyms and their meanings. Refer to this as your Glossary. (In the Unit 1 examination, you may be asked to expand acronyms.)
- In the same notebook, create a personalised Digital Technology dictionary. Include every technical term and write a definition in your own words. In the examinations, you may be asked to explain or describe key terms.
- Developing skills in using generic software packages will help you identify and explain their main features and functions in an examination situation.
- Techniques such as spider diagrams can greatly assist revision as they give you a picture of what you are learning and increase your chances of correctly answering questions.
- Use the CCEA microsite to access past papers and mark schemes so that you become familiar with the structure and layout of the examination. Familiarity will help you settle quickly during the examination, which will improve your performance.
- For any topic where the specification calls for knowledge of advantages and disadvantages, it is important that you know a range of these.

Preparing for the Unit 4 paper

- Identify the areas in the specification where definitions and explanations of concepts are required. Areas such as 'Contemporary trends in software development' require you to learn about the two programming paradigms and their relative advantages.
- It will help to have experience of a programming environment. Try creating, editing and running programs.

Now test yourself answers and glossary at www.hoddereducation.co.uk/myrevisionnotes

- Practise using programming constructs. It is important that you can apply them appropriately to solve a problem. You should know how to use an IF statement or a loop to create a solution.
- You should be able to describe how the different methods of searching and sorting work. Create programs to sort and search a set of numbers using the different methods.
- Designing, creating and running programs to solve a variety of problems will improve your ability to create logical solutions.

Success in the examinations

A well-organised answer to each question, making good use of technical terminology, will help you gain marks. The following points will help you present your best responses to the examiner:

- Review the front cover of the paper and note down or highlight the QWC questions. You are expected to use technical terminology in all your answers, but this is particularly important in QWC questions. Look for hints in the question stem about what structure the examiner expects you to use. Write your answer in full sentences.
- Read each question carefully and highlight the key terms and/or context of the question so you are clear what the examiner expects from you.
- Read the entire question before attempting to answer any part of it. Often candidates provide detailed responses to early parts of a question, only to find their answer is too long and contains content which answers a later part of the same question, further down the page.
- Look at the number of marks and the space given for your answer. (For example, a question worth 1 mark might have 1 line for your response, and so on.) The mark allocation and the amount of space suggest how much you need to write.
- In longer questions, the examiner will expect you to make a range of valid technical points, one for each mark. Therefore, to gain full marks in a question worth 4 marks you need to make 4 clearly stated, relevant points.
- Think about the context of the question, where applicable, and make sure that you refer to the context in your answer, using relevant examples.
- When the question requires more than one example, ensure that you are providing two distinct examples and not simply restating the same point in a different way.
- Use technical terminology and avoid generic terms like 'fast' or 'efficient'.
- Try to write clearly and legibly.
- If you need to continue an answer somewhere else on the paper, mark this clearly at the end of the answer space, and indicate to the examiner where they will find the rest of your response.
- Answer all the questions.

Practice questions and commentary

Unit 1

Sample question 1

Describe two tasks carried out by utility applications software. (6 marks)

> **High-level response**
>
> Disc Defragmentation. This rearranges the data stored on a hard disc so that files are stored in adjacent blocks. It also ensures the free storage spaces are altogether.
>
> Task Scheduling. This involves the processor time being divided amongst a number of tasks. It uses time slices and is implemented using a 'round robin' method.

Commentary

Marks awarded: 5/6

- Two tasks are clearly described.
- Answers are complete.
- Good use of technical terms.

> **Low-level response**
>
> Disc Defragmentation. The data stored on a hard disc is stored together.
>
> Task Scheduling. It uses time slices and each task is given a time slice.

Commentary

Marks awarded: 3/6

- Two tasks are correctly stated.
- Brief descriptions with a lack of clarity, such as '…stored together'.
- Some technical terms included.

Sample question 2

Using an example, describe the following data validation techniques:

1 Range Check
2 Format Check. (4 marks)

> **High-level response**
>
> Range Check. Ensures the data value must be between a lower level and an upper level, such the month in a date of birth between 1 and 12.
>
> Format Check. Ensures the data follows a preset pattern, such as a date of birth being DDMMYYYY.

Commentary

Marks awarded: 4/4

- The two validation checks are clearly described.
- Answers are complete, including a good example in each case.
- Good use of concise language.

Low-level response

Range Check. Ensures the data value is in the range, such as the month in a date of birth between 1 and 12.

Format Check. Ensures the data is in the correct format, such as a date of birth being DDMMYYYY.

Commentary

Marks awarded: 2/4

- The two validation checks are not described; the answers only include words from the question.
- Marks are given for including good examples.

Sample question 3

Evaluate the use of online banking for both the customer and the bank.
(6 marks, QWC question)

High-level response

Online banking allows customers to access their bank account using the Internet. This is done by using a username and password to log on to the website. Transactions can be done at home, work or on the move using mobile technology 24/7. The main drawback of online banking for customers is their concerns about fraud. For the bank fewer branches and staff are required as this can save money. Banks can produce e-statements, which save on paper and postage costs. The main disadvantage for the bank is the need to implement and maintain complex network security systems for customer data.

Commentary

Marks awarded: 5/6

- The answer considers both the customer and the bank.
- The answer includes both advantages and disadvantages for both the customer and the bank, making it a high-level response to an evaluation question.
- Good use of technical terms and QWC.

Low-level response

Cutomers use a username and pasword to log on to the website. For additional security, customers will also be asked a security question(s). A number of activities are available from viewing transactions and bank statments to setting up regular payments using drect debits/standing orders. Customers can use the bank all day everyday.

Commentary

Marks awarded: 2/6

- The answer only focuses on the customer, with no reference to the bank.
- The answer includes features of online banking instead of focusing on evaluating it.
- Some credit is awarded for giving an advantage for the customer.
- Reasonable QWC but there are a few spelling errors.

Unit 2

REVISED

Sample question 1

Social media applications make use of interactive features. Describe two interactive features used in social media applications and explain how they can help enhance the user's online experience. (6 marks, QWC question)

> **Level 3 response**
>
> 1) Live streaming is a recent and popular feature of many social media applications. They allow the user to record and post live video content which can be shared with their social media followers. This allows the user of the social media account to share their thoughts, ideas and experiences immediately with their followers without worrying about spending time having to type commentary. It gives their followers a true image of who they are.
>
> 2) Users can use their social media account to post links to content from other applications they or someone else has posted on other internet sites. The users can create and share a wide range of content with their followers and by posting the link to the other site or application they followers can locate additional related content by clicking on the link.

Commentary

Marks awarded: 5/6

- Two methods are clearly described.
- Good technical terminology is used.
- The answer contains a description of how each interactive feature can enhance the user's online experience.

> **Level 2 response**
>
> 1) Live streaming can be used to add live video to a social media account and other users can view your video at any time.
>
> 2) Multimedia links can be added to any post made on a multimedia account. When the user clicks on the link it will take them to another website.

Commentary

Marks awarded: 4/6

- Two methods are described.
- Some technical terminology is used.
- The answer describes the interactive features but does not explain how they can enhance the user's online experience.

Sample question 2

Many website developers use web authoring applications. Place a tick beside two statements which correctly describe the advantages of web authoring applications. (2 marks)

1 Little technical knowledge is needed; professional applications can be produced with little programming knowledge.

2 Updated links: links are not updated automatically when the content is moved between folders using the management tool.

3 The interface is intuitive; this leads to fast application development as elements can be easily placed on screen using appropriate tools.

4 Limited options are available and the developer may have to code some elements of the application if interactivity is required.

> **High-level response**
>
> Statements 1 and 3 were ticked.

Commentary

Marks awarded: 2/2

Two options are clearly and correctly selected. (If the candidate had selected one correct option and one incorrect option, they would have been awarded only one mark.)

> **Low-level response**
>
> Statements 1, 2 and 3 were ticked.

Commentary

Marks awarded: 1/2

- The two correct options were ticked, so two marks were given for this.
- BUT the candidate also ticked a third, incorrect response: one mark was subtracted for this. (If the candidate had selected even more of the incorrect responses, they could lose more marks to a minimum of zero marks.)

Sample question 3

Eimear has created a website for her Technology and Design homework. The home page and the HTML code used to display it are shown below.

```
<!DOCTYPE HTML PUBLIC>
<html>
<head>
<meta http-equiv="Content-Type" content="text/html;
charset=iso-8859-1">
<title>Home Page</title>
</head>

<body>
 <p><h1>History of the Car<\h1>
 <p><img src="media/Picture1.png" width ="500" height="333"></p>
 </p>
 <p> <a href="Mass production.htm">Mass Production</a>
<a href="Brass Era.htm">Brass Era</a>
<a href="Classic Era.htm">Classic Era</a>
<a href="Modern Era.htm">Modern Era</a>

 <p>My website on the history of the Car will look at four main points in
the history of the motor car. I will look at</p>

 <p>How cars were mass produced</p>
 <p>What cars looked like during the Brass Era</p>
 <p>What cars looked like in the Classic Era</p>
 <p>How cars have changed in the Modern Era</p>

</body>
</html>
```

Part (a)

Eimear wants to display the text in lines 20 to 23 with a bullet point at the start of each line. In the table below, circle the HTML code option which will display the text in this manner. (1 mark)

Option 1	Option 2	Option 3

<ol>
 	
  <li>How cars were mass produced</li>
 	
  <li>What cars looked like during the Brass Era</li>
 	
  <li>What cars looked like in the Classic Era</li>
 	
  <li>How cars have changed in the Modern Era </li>
 	
 </ol>
	<ul>
	
	  <li>How cars were mass produced</li>
	
	  <li>What cars looked like during the Brass Era</li>
	
	  <li>What cars looked like in the Classic Era</li>
	
	  <li>How cars have changed in the Modern Era </li>
	
	 </ul>
		<ul>
		
		  <li>How cars were mass produced
		
		  What cars looked like during the Brass Era
		
		  What cars looked like in the Classic Era
		
		  How cars have changed in the Modern Era </li>
		
		  </ul>

Commentary

- Option 1 will display the text as an ordered list where each item in the list will be numbered.

- Option 2 is the correct answer; it will display the text as a list with 4 items, each starting with a bullet point.

- Option 3 will display the text as a single line of text with a bullet point at the beginning. In order to display the content on four separate lines the <li> </li> tags would be needed to show the start and end of each list item.

Part (b)

Eimear amends the HTML code on line 10 so it now reads:

```
<p><img src="media/Picture1.png" width="500" height="333" alt="car image"></p>
```

Explain the purpose of the alt tag when displaying images. (2 marks)

High-level response

The alt tag is used to specify alternative text for an image if the image cannot be displayed by the browser, or if the user is using a screen reader it will read a description of the image to them. Some browsers will display the alternative text for the user if they roll over the image with their mouse.

Commentary

Marks awarded: 2/2

- A full description of the purpose of the tag is provided (i.e. that the tag provides alternative text).
- Technical terminology is used.
- A detailed outline of the reason for including the alt tag with the image tag is also provided.

Medium-level response

Alt is used to provide additional text to help describe an on-screen image.

Commentary

Marks awarded: 1/2

- A brief description of the purpose of the tag is provided.
- Technical terminology in the answer is limited.
- There is no explanation why the tag is used in this context, so the second mark cannot be awarded.

Unit 4

REVISED

Sample question 1

Testing is an important aspect of system development. Explain two ways in which a software application can be tested to ensure it is a robust solution. (6 marks, QWC question)

Level 3 response

1) White box testing is carried out on units of code and involves detailed testing of the internal logic of the program. It identifies errors in syntax, logic and data flow. A programmer will carry this out and the testing will test every pathway in the code. In this type of testing, hidden errors are identified and the code is then modified and optimised.

2) Black box testing focuses in inputs and outputs. It is used to identify errors in data structures, problems with user interfaces, missing functionality and behaviour errors. The tester does not need any knowledge about the internal code. A variety of users will carry out this type of testing. This type of testing can help identify where the user requirements are not being met.

Commentary

Marks awarded: 5/6

- Two methods of testing are clearly described.
- Good technical terminology is used.
- The answer contains a description of how each type of testing contributes to the robustness of the system.

Level 2 response

1) White box testing is carried out on units of code it shows errors in syntax, logic and data flow. A programmer will carry out and the testing. .

2) Black box testing is used to identify errors in user interfaces and missing functions. The tester does not need any knowledge about the internal code.

Commentary

Marks awarded: 3/6

- Two methods are described.
- Some technical terminology is used.
- The answer contains a description of the testing but does not describe how each type of testing contributes to the robustness of the system.

Sample question 2

Place a tick beside two statements which are true about Object-Oriented Programming (OOP). (2 marks)

1 OOP makes use of classes which define properties and methods for objects.

2 OOP relies on implementing procedures and a top-down approach to design is used.

3 OOP makes use of step-by-step solutions coded as functions which perform tasks on data.

4 OOP makes use of inheritance, which allows classes to inherit characteristics from parent or super classes.

> **High-level response**
>
> Statements 1 and 4 are ticked.

Commentary

Marks awarded: 2/2

Two options are clearly and correctly selected. (If the candidate had selected one correct option and one incorrect option, they would have been awarded only one mark.)

> **Low-level response**
>
> Statements 1, 2, 3 and 4 are ticked.

Commentary

Marks awarded: 0/2

Two correct options have been ticked by the candidate BUT the candidate has also ticked two incorrect options, for which marks are subtracted.

Sample question 3

A company supplies and delivers presentation boxes to customers. The price of the box depends on the size and shape provided and the number of boxes ordered.

Type of box	Price
Box type 1: Small square	£0.50
Box type 2: Large square	£0.75
Box type 3: Small circle	£0.50
Box type 4: Large circle	£0.75
Box type 5: Octagonal	£1.00

A variable called boxType has been declared. It will store the type of box required by a customer. This must be validated to ensure it is between 1 and 5. Write an algorithm which will validate the boxType. (4 marks)

Practice questions and commentary

High-level response

```
do { okFlag = true;
      Console.Write("Enter Box Type in the range 1-5 \t");
      boxType = Convert.ToInt32(Console.ReadLine());
      if ((boxType < 1) || (boxType > 5))
        { Console.WriteLine("Error - out of range");
        okFlag = false; [
    } while (okFlag == false);
```

Commentary

Marks awarded: 4/4

- 1 mark for flag assignment (line 1).
- 1 mark for IF condition (line 4).
- 1 mark for flag re-assignment (line 6).
- 1 mark for loop condition (line 7).

The candidate has created an algorithm that correctly reads the boxType variable and sets a Boolean variable based on the value input. The range check is correct and the loop condition will continue until a value in the correct range is entered.

Low-level response

```
do {
      Console.Write("Enter Box Type in the range 1-5 \t");
      boxType = Convert.ToInt32(Console.ReadLine( ));
      if ((boxType <= 1) || (boxType > 5))
      { Console.WriteLine("Error - out of range");
        okFlag = false;
    } while (okFlag == false);
```

Commentary

Marks awarded: 2/4

- No mark for flag assignment: flag is not set at start of loop.
- No mark for IF condition.
- 1 mark for flag re-assignment (line 6).
- 1 mark for loop condition (line 7).

The candidate has created an algorithm which correctly reads the boxType variable, but it does not set a Boolean variable based on the value input. The range check is incorrect. The loop condition is correct, but the loop will continue endlessly as the flag is not set at the start of the loop.